LIFE IN THE PAST LANE

VOLUME TWO

A LOOK INTO MEDIA HISTORY THROUGH
THE EYES OF THOSE WHO MADE IT!

BY JASON HILL

LIFE IN THE PAST LANE—VOLUME TWO
©2015 Jason Hill

All rights reserved.

No part of this book may be reproduced in any form or by any means, electronic, mechanical, digital, photocopying, or recording, except for in the inclusion of a review, without permission in writing from the publisher.

Published in the USA by:

BearManor Media
P.O. Box 71426
Albany, Georgia 31708
www.BearManorMedia.com

ISBN-10: 1-59393-781-4 (alk. paper)
ISBN-13: 978-1-59393-781-2 (alk. paper)

Design and Layout: Valerie Thompson

TABLE OF CONTENTS

ACKNOWLEDGMENTS 1

FOREWORD/PROGRAM NOTES 3

INTRODUCTION/OVERTURE 5

    A LITTLE EARLY HISTORY OF THE BBC

ACT I: THE BRITISH ARE COMING 9

    Interview with Max Geldray

ACT II: THE BRITISH HAVE COME 29

    Talk with Alan Young

ACT III: BRIDGES UP! 49

    SCENE ONE: THROCKMORTON THE SECOND 51

    Discussion with Willard Waterman—Wisconsin, Chicago and beyond

    SCENE TWO: RADIO IDOL 73

    Chat with Les Tremayne—London to Chicago to Hollywood

    SCENE THREE: FROM TENTS TO HOLLYWOOD 87

    Olan Soulé speaks about his long and varied career

ACT IV: MORE CHICAGO CONNECTIONS 101

SCENE ONE: WISTFUL VISTA 103

Conversation with Jim Jordan—from Peoria to major comedy

SCENE TWO: K, F, & O 123

Conferring with Fran Allison—the Queen of Ad-lib

PHOTO GALLERY 137

ACT V: NEW YORK, NEW YORK 177

SCENE ONE: YOU SAID WHAT? 179

Talking with Henry Morgan.

SCENE TWO: GERARD 197

Interview with Arnold Stang

SCENE THREE: SATIRIC JESTERS 211

Having some fun with Bob Elliot and Ray Goulding (Bob and Ray)

ACT VI: WILD, WILD WEST 129

SCENE ONE: NOT JUST A COWBOY 131

The words of John Dehner—He did it all.

SCENE TWO: FROM THE CIRCUS TO THE PLAINS 257

Parley Baer tells us what it was like to be Chester Proudfoot

ACT VII: KEEPING US INFORMED 277

Discussion about Edward R. Murrow with Ann Sperber, author of *Murrow, His Life and Times*

ACT VIII: NETWORK IMPRESARIO 303
  Biography of William S. Paley in the words of Lew Paper,
  Author of *Empire: William S. Paley and the Making of CBS*

AFTERWORD/FINALE 319

BIBLIOGRAPHY 323

INDEX 325

DEDICATION

For Tish
She gave so much for so long.

Acknowledgments

There are so many people involved in the production of any published work it would be impossible to name them all. First, I must thank the people at BearManor Media who coordinated this project, Ben Ohmart, Michelle Morgan and Crystal Grabman. Much credit must also go to Valerie Thompson for her work in assembling the final printed copy.

Without a doubt, this book would not have happened without the aid of my inimitable final word editor and friend, Michaela Nelson, not only for her work with my copy, but also for preventing me several times from throwing my laptop at the wall when it tried to write its own version. I must also thank Paula Slade for her knowledgeable advice on the process.

Last, but not least, I have to thank all of the people whose words made up the bulk of this work. In truth, they were the ones who wrote it.

J. H.

Foreword/ Program Notes

When thinking about media history, there are many different aspects to consider. We must look at a variety of separate, but distinct types of entertainment formats. The one that this volume will deal with mostly, but not exclusively, is radio.

During the course of my career I spent several years working in that particular medium, first as an audio engineer and later as a broadcaster. At that time I began to notice that, while many stations were airing a plethora of old radio shows from the Golden Years, not many of them were doing the one thing that brought those programs to life. I decided to remedy that situation by doing a series of extensive interviews with many of the multi-talented folks who made radio tick from its onset until its unfortunate ultimate demise.

I created a show called *Life in the Past Lane* and very soon discovered that there was a definite audience for the information many of my guests imparted about their shows and, more importantly, about themselves as well. I went into great depth with each and every participant during the project, which took place over twenty-five years ago. The good news is that I still have copies of all of those long discussions. The bad news is that nearly all of my guests have since passed on making it impossible to offer any additional updated information.

What I will present here are transcriptions of a few of those many, many conversations so that they will not be lost when I, too, am gone.

My own personal history runs concurrent with that of radio. During my formative years, I was one of the most avid listeners to a great many of those broadcasts. For me, radio is like a long, lost child. Much of it was very, very good while some of it was just plain awful.

Read on and listen to some of the voices from that enchanted past, a time that I dearly miss. Nothing of its ilk will ever be again, so let us delve into a bit of what remains of the "Theatre of the Mind."

INTRODUCTION/OVERTURE: A LITTLE EARLY HISTORY OF THE BBC

I think it is appropriate, before getting into the meat of this volume, to say a few words about a very important subject. That subject is the BBC, The British Broadcasting Corporation. It is the most widespread network on the face of our planet and had a great deal to do with my first two guests herein.

Murmurs of this huge corporation were detected as early as the later part of the 19th century, but for this short piece we will just consider their actual beginnings on the air as a group.

It is truly astounding that the BBC ever got off square one, due to the crushing rules they had to work with before their first broadcast became a reality. That broadcast was on October 10, 1922. The original company was formed by combining six equipment manufacturers, each one fighting for overall control.

Prior to that time, each ran a separate operation with limited success because of the restrictions put on them. First of all, the whole radio business was under the control of the Postmaster General. He did not see eye to eye with any of the people who were attempting to get started in what was then a very new industry. They were not allowed to report any news that had not already been printed in the daily papers. They were also not permitted to have any music or advertising.

To further complicate matters, there were severe limitations on broadcast time. On-air time could not exceed one hour per day. That hour could be either between eleven a.m. and noon or between two and four p.m. To make matters worse, there had to be a break every seven minutes to make announcements. Those breaks usually turned out to be dead air, which would be anathema in today's market place.

There were a few notable exceptions. One of those was a concert performed by Dame Nellie Melba on June 15, 1920 for the Marconi Company. It was heard in parts of Europe and as far away as Newfoundland. Since they were working with what was mainly telephone equipment that was pretty impressive.

By the time the British Broadcasting Company, Ltd. was formed in 1922, some of the more stringent rules and regulations had been lifted. Hours on the air could be as many as seven daily between five p.m. and midnight and music was permitted on a regular basis.

The six companies that united to begin the illustrious history of the BBC were The Marconi Company, which actually made its first appearance in 1901, The General Electric Company, The Radio Communications Company, The Metropolitan-Vickers Company, usually referred to as Metrovick, The Western Electric Company, and The British Thompson-Houston Company. The main objective of all of them was to sell receiving equipment; therefore, they had to produce some programming to be received.

The first five stations that made up the new network during 1922 were scattered throughout the British Isles. They were 2LO from London, 2ZY from Manchester, 5IT from Birmingham, 2WP also originally from London but later moved, 2MT from Chelmsford and 5NO from Newcastle. In 1923 they were joined by five more. Those were 5WR from Cardiff, 5SC from Glasgow, 2BD from Aberdeen, 6BM from Bournemouth and 6FL from Sheffield. Getting into the act in 1924 were ten more. Some of them were relay stations to augment the coverage. Added during that year were 2BE from Belfast, 5PY from Plymouth, 2EH from Edinburgh, 6LV from Liverpool, 2LS from Leeds and Bradford, 6KH from Hull, 5NG from Nottingham, 2DE from Dundee, 6ST from Stoke-on-Trent and finally, 5SX from Swansea.

If you are at all familiar with the territory, you can see that they had it all pretty well covered. It included England, Scotland, Ireland, and Wales, but that was only the beginning. As time went by they developed assets all over the globe. It was not long before several magazines came on the market, which were devoted entirely to radio.

From the very start there were always attempts made to measure the size of the audience. Here is an example of what they did. At 2MT there was an engineer, who was also a broadcaster, named

Peter Eckersley. He once did a show called *A Night of Grand Opera*. When that show was finished, he sang the following:

Dearest, the concert's ended. Sad wails the heterodyne.
You must switch off your valves. I must soon switch off mine.
Write back and say you heard me, your hook-up, where and how.
Quick, for the engine's failing. Goodbye, you old low-brow.

I do not know what the response was. You must admit he used some grit along with wit.

On the first day of 1927 an important change took place that exists to this day. That was the day when the first Royal Charter was signed taking control out of the hands of the post office. That was when the name was changed to what we know it to be now, The British Broadcasting Corporation. Those charters have continued through the years, being renewed every decade until the current charter, which will run until 2016. Until 1955 the BBC operated as a monopoly with no competition. Fifty-five is when the ITV channel came on the air, but that is another story altogether.

The British Empire may be a thing of the past, but the BBC is alive and well and continues to grow.

I have only touched on a few salient points from the beginning of a very long and intriguing story. To learn much, much more I suggest that you read any of the books written by Asa Briggs on the subject. In 1985, he published one titled *The BBC: The First Fifty Years*. It is still available and well worth the time to read it.

As I have said, it is amazing that they ever got their show on the road.

ACT I:
THE BRITISH
ARE COMING

Before venturing into domestic broadcasting, I think it might be fun to travel across the pond and pay a visit on the BBC, one of the oldest and most respected networks in our world. Their reach is global; with outlets in some places we only read about in geography books or find in an atlas. They have always maintained certain decorum, no matter where they were heard. The "King's English" is what they spoke. Their announcers were made of very strict cloth. That is not to say that some of the programs themselves could not cut loose from those apron strings and simply go hog wild from time to time.

What I offer now is a perfect example of freeing those restraints, and, for the most part, ridiculing their revered heritage. It was something that, while it had happened before to some degree, had never reached the level of zaniness that it did on *The Goon Show*. Interestingly enough, that particular program proved to be a favorite venue of the Royal Family, proving that the British are not above laughing at themselves.

In more recent times, on television, there have been many more examples of that sort of demeanor, most notably, *Monty Python*, but *The Goon Show* was the true groundbreaker of that form of insanity.

Reaching out to try to make contact with any one of the members of that outrageous cast, I finally struck gold. Although Peter Sellers had passed away in 1980 and the other two principles, Harry Secombe and Spike Milligan, were unreachable, due to extensive travel schedules, I did manage to find a man who was an integral part of all of the *Goon Show* performances. We spoke at length on May 7, 1986 and he had much to say.

His name was Max Geldray.

****

JASON: Max, your background wasn't originally with the BBC. You worked earlier on the continent, having been born in Holland.

MAX: I was born in Holland, and I did my very first radio broadcast in Holland in 1934.

JASON: And that must have been on Radio Hilversum?

MAX: Yes, Hilversum One.

JASON: Which is the main radio outlet in Holland—in fact, the only outlet. You were living in Bilthoven at the time, right?

MAX: That's actually where I was brought up. That's where I had my schooling. Of course, I was born in Amsterdam.

JASON: I'm very familiar with Bilthoven. I lived just a few miles down the road, in Baarn during part of the fifties when I was working for KLM. You are a harmonica player, jazz harmonica?

MAX: I was the first jazz harmonica player in Europe.

JASON: Which was a real specialty, something we don't hear much anymore.

MAX: No, and you certainly didn't hear it then. When I did my first broadcast I was very good according to the critics, but when you figure that nobody else was doing it, I didn't have much opposition. I was unique, if you like.

JASON: Like saying, "He's fine, but compared to what"?

MAX: Yes, right. I was very lucky nobody else was doing it. I was king of my own domain.

JASON: You played a lot of club dates all over Europe and also in England. I believe you eventually ended up joining Ray Ventura while you were in France.

MAX: That was several years later after I'd paid my dues in the clubs, particularly in Belgium. I used to play harmonica in a club, just like it was another instrument, many hours a night, seven nights a week. It gave me a lot of schooling.

JASON: Somewhere along the way you met Django Reinhardt. Was that in Paris?

MAX: Yes, when I was working with Ray Ventura in Paris I got acquainted with *The Hot Club de France* and saw Django playing with the *Hot Club Quartet*. You might be aware of Stephan Grappelli, his violinist.

JASON: I met Stephan when he was on tour and played Madison last year. He's doing well and still sounds great. It wasn't until after the war that you actually ended up in England.

MAX: Well, I went to England in 1937 for a six-week tour. That was my first connection with England. Then I went back to Holland. Then I got into the clubs in Belgium and when the war started, I escaped to England. That is when the connection started. I was in the army during the war.

JASON: But your actual connection with the BBC was after the war?

MAX: My actual connection with the BBC started before the war, because, when I was with Ray Ventura we did the very first television broadcast, when it was still experimental. That's how I got connected with the BBC and got to know people there. When I got back after the war they put me on every possible type of variety broadcast. When I went back to England after the war I did a lot of broadcasts before *The Goon Show* started. Pat Dixon, the guy who later became the producer of *The Goon Show*, took a liking to me. He always liked my playing. He was about the only producer on the BBC who always called me after every broadcast I did and said, "That was really great, Max." One day I said to him, "You're the only producer that compliments me on my work, but you're also the only one who has never given me a broadcast on the BBC." He answered, "When I do give you a broadcast it will be the best you ever had." Funny enough, what we called a trial recording, which you here call a pilot, it was from him. It was *The Goon Show*. Low and behold, *The Goon Show* became a ten-year gig.

JASON: And those shows are still being rerun somewhere around the planet these days.

MAX: Yep!

JASON: BBC radio is still geared to drama and comedy more than anything we know in this country. *The Goon Show* is mainly what this discussion is about, because you were a 'regular' on it. It's a show that, whenever it's played here, people listen to it and say, "What was that," or something along those lines. The humor moves so fast and some of it is too British to be understood by Americans, but if you really listen closely, it is one of the funniest shows ever put together.

MAX: And you know, Jason, I run into people, I would say on a monthly basis, every month since I've been in this country, twenty five years, I always run into someone who knows *The Goon Show*. People who come from Australia, for instance, or from other English speaking countries. I talked to a friend of mine one day and mentioned *The Goon Show*. He said that while he was a prisoner of war they used to play *The Goon Show* tapes. I think that was about the most original that I've heard. The other thing that's always amazed me is that while we were broadcasting *The Goon Show*, the British navy would stop whatever they were doing. When that half hour came on they were all listening, the whole crew. As crazy as that show was, it was so popular. In the beginning, the BBC itself didn't know what was going on. I think there may have been plans to take it off the air after a little while. Then they started to notice that the studio was always packed with very influential people, people like Winston Churchill, people like the Royal Family. They decided that if those people liked it, there must be something to it.

JASON: I have an article in front of me from *The Sunday Times* from December 1957 titled "Goonland in danger." The main thrust of the piece is exactly what you just said. I do know that it was the favorite of many of the royals. Let's talk about some of the people who were on the show with you. First, we should talk about the music end because that was your main concern. Ray Ellington was always featured in one break and you in the other. Ray occasionally played a small part or two in the body of the show too, didn't he?

MAX: Amazingly, yes. Both of us used to do that, but Ray had the most identifiable part.

Jason: Of course, the main people from the comedy standpoint were Peter Sellers, Harry Secombe and Spike Milligan. I believe Spike is still active.

Max: Oh, yeah, in fact, I talked to him just a few days ago. He told me he was on his way to Australia right now where he's going to do a play. There's also a chance that he may come to this country because he has a part in some film. He's still writing as well. He writes children's books.

Jason: He wrote most of *The Goon* shows.

Max: Spike was definitely the main writer. It was a difficult show to write. It was very hard on him. Not only was he in the show, he more or less directed everything to get it the way he wrote it. Now and then he had some co-writers. Everybody had something to do with it, so he had input from several people, but he stood the brunt of it.

Jason: Spike, Peter, and Harry all came together at the Windmill Theatre. I would think that was the first place they would have been together. That's where the whole thing started. Harry was working at the Windmill after the war. I think the other two went to visit him while he was working there and that's where it all began.—Also, Michael Bentine at that time.

Max: They were in the army together, too. That's where it really began.

Jason: Let me read a short piece that Spike wrote. It's the description of a character he played on the show. Anybody who is new to *The Goon Show* should get a rough idea of what it was about from these few lines.

Born in 1863, the only child of Ethel Cox—virgin birth—educated at convent until the age of seven—end of education—had 15,312 interviews for jobs and has never been employed—spends his days walking around saying, 'Hello Dere' to anyone who will listen—wears a thirty-three year old Burton suit and is occasionally used by the Metropolitan Police for target practice.

It goes on from there, but that's enough to convey the concept.

MAX: The sound of the man was a little like Mortimer Snerd. There was a funny bit where Eccles was supposed to be helping someone back up a truck. He keeps on going, "Okay, okay." So the truck keeps going back and all of the sudden there is this enormous crash. When the crash is over and everything has fallen down, he realized the truck has driven into the building. The whole building came down. It all goes quiet and you hear Eccles quietly say, "Stop!"

JASON: That's just the sort of thing that made *The Goon Show* what it was. You just brought up another point by describing a building coming down. Sound effects where a tremendous part of the show and, in fact, the sounds that were called for stretched what was assumed to be the largest sound library in the world.

MAX: A lot of the sound effects were on records in those days instead of tape. It was records, if you still remember that.

JASON: They still are.

MAX: While much of it was on records, there were also

added sound effects done right there on the stage while we were doing the shows. Eventually, we did our show in a famous old theatre which was bought by the BBC, the Camden Theatre. The sound effects man and sometimes two sound effects men, plus the pre-recorded stuff, was going on, and the audience would sometimes roll in the aisles because of the sound men. They were running around hitting things and throwing things all over the place to match the script.

JASON: I remember seeing other shows in Chicago in the forties with live sound effects, so I know what you're saying. In the case of *The Goon Show*, the sounds were often exaggerated forty fold over what was on those old shows done here. Peter Sellers was a man who played quite a few parts on your show. The names of the characters were funny enough standing alone. He played a couple of the goons, Bluebottle and Willum. He also played Major Dennis Bloodnok, Gravely Headstone, Cyril Crincinknutt and many others.

MAX: Henry Crun, Prunella Dirt, there was a whole list of them.

JASON: One of them was very hard to pronounce, Lance Brigadier Hercules Grytpype Thynne. They used to run over that name very quickly, but it's not easy to say quickly. Harry Secombe was mainly Neddy Seagoon and occasionally some other characters, but Neddy was the main character on the show. People in this country may not be familiar with Harry, but he has done several films here, one of which was *Oliver*. We talked earlier about Spike. He shows up every once in a while on American television. He was a guest on *The Muppet Show* a few years ago and no one there understood him either, because he was doing Spike Milligan. The announcer, Bill, always got the brunt of their strange humor. His real name was Wallace Greenslade. There was always a bit at the start of every program. He would say, "This is the *BBC* home service." Then a voice would come in and say, "Is there no mercy?"—or something like that. It was a little different on each occasion. They were always picking on poor Bill and the station and the network. Their description of their main objectives was, first, to destroy the BBC, then the British Commonwealth and finally, the whole world, with laughs of course.

MAX: Let me tell you a little about Wallace Greenslade, because I think that was another first in broadcasting and particularly on the BBC. You will note that Wallace was quite a typical BBC announcer who would never say anything wrong. The BBC used to be, and I'm sure still is, very strict about their announcers when it came to reading things. It had to be all perfect. This man had a very perfect British voice. Then they used him on *The Goon Show* and made him say awful stuff. Since he was a large man he was also something to behold among all the commotion. He was perfectly dressed while all the rest of us were in casual clothes, so unless one knows the British type of announcer, it would not have been funny. To hear a British announcer say crazy things was, in itself, hilarious.

JASON: That's another whole area altogether. The BBC was very particular about using what had once been called "The King's English" and later was called "BBC English," because it isn't really the way the language is spoken on the streets of London. Their news broadcasts around the world were probably the main reason for it. It would be

	universal. People could readily understand it anywhere.
MAX:	Are you aware that there was another announcer before Wallace?
JASON:	I am not.
MAX:	Timothy was his first name. He was even more a typical BBC announcer and even more rigid. He had a dislike for *The Goons.* He left the show, but much later he came back. The final show that we did was for the 50th anniversary of the BBC. They used Timothy for the show and he was tremendous. It was called, "The Last Goon Show of All." It was always done with a live audience, but it wasn't broadcast live.
	We always did it on Sunday at six o'clock. I myself had a strange thing happen. In those days all of us were working vaudeville and we would work together very often. Peter and I used to go into a theatre somewhere in Briton or Scotland or Wales or where ever. We always had to be back on Sunday afternoons to do the show. One day I had a car accident. My car flipped over on the ice. The only thing that happened to me was that I got a very bad swollen lip. It couldn't have been my finger. It had to be my lip, not good for a harmonica player. Someone took me to the show. I was able to do it on the side of my mouth. It was funny to the audience. It wasn't funny for me. One time when Peter and I were doing a theatre in one of the towns in England, we were working on the stage. I would do my act, and then Peter would do his. I would close the first half of the show and Peter would close the second. Peter Sellers never liked being on the stage alone. Very often, in order to do

part of his required time, he would do part of his act during my act. He would just wander onto stage. He might find some old hat and pull it over his eyes and maybe an old raincoat. All of the sudden, I would find him standing at the side of the stage while I was trying to do my part. He would just shuffle onto the stage.

On one occasion he showed up on the stage and people didn't know what was going on. He came right up to me and said, in a strange voice, "What is this theatre?" I said to him, "Don't you know, this is the beautiful Empire Theatre in Over-Hampton." He stood there and looked around. You have to understand, some of those theatres really needed some repair, because it was very near the end of vaudeville, or variety as we called it. America had already given up on vaudeville for a long time, but in England it was still going on. At that time it was losing its interest. Peter looked around again after I told him where we were and saw that it was a little shabby. All of the sudden he said, in his peculiar voice, "It could do with a good old burn." That's a typical English way of saying it. It was a Saturday night that he said that. Peter and I went back to London in one car to do *The Goon Show*. Sunday morning he called me up and he said, "Guess what happened? I just heard on the news that the theatre in Over-Hampton burned down last night."

JASON: Oops, that sounds suspicious.

MAX: We did say, "Did we give them an idea?"

****

The hilarious Goons are all gone now. We lost Peter Sellers in 1980; Michael Bentine, who had been one of the original Goons, in 1996; Harry Secombe in 2001; Spike Milligan in 2002 and Max Geldray in 2004.

With them went all those endearing characters they had created. Gone is Minnie Bannister, gone is Sergeant Throat, gone are Major Bloodnak and Flowerdew and Private Bogg, and Izzy, and all the rest. Yes, they are all gone but they will never be forgotten. In his declining years Spike jokingly said that he hoped that Harry would die before him so he would be unable to sing at Spike's funeral. The odd thing is that even though Harry preceded Spike to the grave he still sang at Spike's funeral—on tape. It was a typical "Goon" thing.

The Goon Show has been described in many ways. It has been called four dimensional, surrealist and avant-garde. It was also dubbed an audio cartoon.

I had the very distinct pleasure to produce, direct, and engineer a remake of one of the many scripts that remain—with a far different cast. The one we did was "The Dreaded Batter Pudding Hurler." It was not the easiest thing to get the actors to be zany enough to approximate the original, but, in the end, it came out well.

I think it would be appropriate to end this piece with a direct quote from Con Mahoney, head of light entertainment for radio at the BBC, about the origin of *The Goon Show*.

He said, *"Historians of the future will find it difficult to lay responsibility for the Goons on any one doorstep. A Westminster hostelry, 'The Grafton Arms', could well, at some time in the future, carry a blue plaque to the effect that 'Goonery was brewed here.'"*

Wherever and whenever it really began, radio archives would be decidedly poorer had it never happened.

****

ENCORE

Before we leave Goondom behind, I cannot resist adding a short sample of how it sounded. Here is the opening scene from "The Dreaded Batter Pudding Hurler," for those of you who are unfamiliar with the show.

GREENSLADE: This is the BBC Home Service.

(Penny in mug)

GREENSLADE: Thank you. We now come to the radio show entirely dedicated to the downfall of John Snagge.

SECOMBE: He, of course, refers to the highly esteemed Goon Show.

(Funeral dirge with wailing people)

SECOMBE: Stop! Time for laughs later, but now to business. Mr. Greenslade, come over here.

(Rattling chains)

GREENSLADE: Yes master?

SECOMBE: Tell the world what we have for them.

GREENSLADE: My lords and ladies, and national assistance holders—Tonight the League of Burmese Trombonists present a best-selling play entitled:

(Timpani roll)

SELLERS: The Terror of Bexhill-on-Sea, or...

(Trombone chord)

SECOMBE: "The Dreaded Batter Pudding Hurler."

(Sinister horn chord)

GREENSLADE: The English Channel, 1941. Across the silent strip of gray-green water—in England—coastal towns are deserted, except for people. Despite the threat of invasion and the stringent blackout rules, elderly gentlefolk of Bexhill-on-Sea still took their evening constitutionals.

(Sea crashing on beach)

HENRY: Ohhh, dear, dear, ohh, it's quite windy on these cliffs Minnie.

MINNIE: Yes, yes, what a nice summer evening, typical English evening.

HENRY: Mnk, yes, the rain is lovely and warm, Minnie. I think I'll take one of my sou'westers off.

MINNIE: You devil you!

HENRY: Here, Minnie, hold my elephant gun.

MINNIE: Oh, dear, I don't know what you brought it for. You can't shoot elephants in England, you know.

HENRY: Mnk? Why not?

MINNIE: They're out of season.

HENRY: Oh, does that mean we shall have to have pelican for dinner again?

MINNIE: I fear so. I fear so.

HENRY: Then I'll risk it...I'll shoot an elephant out of season.

MINNIE: You can't shoot an elephant out of season.

HENRY: Yes I can, Minnie.

Minnie: Elephants mustn't be shot out of season!

Greenslade: Listeners who are listening will, of course, realize that Minnie and Henry are talking rubbish. As erudite people will realize, there are no elephants in Sussex. They're only found in Kent, north of a line drawn between two points, thus making it the shortest distance.

(Penny in mug)

Greenslade: Thank you!

Henry: Well then, if that's how it is I can't shoot any.

Minnie: Come Henry, we'd better be getting home. I don't want to be caught on the beaches if there's an invasion.

Henry: Neither do I, Minnie. I'm wearing a dirty shirt and I don't...

(Metal door slides open)

Henry: Oh, Oh, Minnie?

Minnie: What, what, what, whatwhatwhatwhat?

Henry: Minnie, did you hear a gas oven door slam just then?

Minnie: Don't be silly. Who'd be walking around these cliffs with a gas oven?

Henry: Lady Docker?

Minnie: Yes, but apart from the obvious ones, who'd want to...

(*Whoosh! Splat!*)

MINNIE: Oooooooooooooooooooooh, Yehhhhhhhhhhhh!

HENRY: No, I've never heard of him.

MINNIE: Help Henry! I've been struck down from behind, help!

HENRY: Mnk—oh dear, dear. Poor Minnie! Police! English Police! Law Guardians!

MINNIE: Not too loud Henry, they'll hear you.

HENRY: Police of the law!

(*Police whistle*)

(*Swoosh*)

SEAGOON: Can I help you, sir?

HENRY: Are you a policeman?

SEAGOON: No, I'm a constable.

HENRY: Oh, what is the difference?

SEAGOON: They're spelt differently.

MINNIE: Oooh, help me differently spelt constable.

SEAGOON: What's happened to this dear old silver bearded lady?

HENRY: She was struck down from behind.

SEAGOON:	And not a moment too soon. Congratulations, sir.
HENRY:	I didn't do it.
SEAGOON:	Coward, hand back your OBE. Now tell me, who did this felonious deed? What's happened to her?
HENRY:	It's much too dark to see. Strike a light.
SEAGOON:	Not allowed in the blackout.
MINNIE:	Strike a dark light.
SEAGOON:	No, madam! Madam, we daren't. Why, only twenty-eight miles across the Channel the Germans are watching this coast.
HENRY:	Don't you be a silly-pilly policeman.
MINNIE:	Bravo, Henry!
HENRY:	Pitty-poo!
MINNIE:	Pitty-poo! They can't see a match being struck.
SEAGOON:	Oh, all right.

(Match strike—bomb whistle—explosion)

SEAGOON:	Any questions?
HENRY:	Yes, where are my legs?
MINNIE:	Where are mine?

SEAGOON: Now, are you aware of German long range guns?

HENRY: Mnk! I have it! I've got it! Just by chance I happen to have a box of German matches.

SEAGOON: Wonderful! Strike one! Ha, they don't dare fire at their own matches.

HENRY: Of course not. Now...

(Strike—whistle—boom)

HENRY: Curse!! The British, the British!

SEAGOON: We tried using a candle, but it wasn't very bright and we daren't light it, so we waited for dawn. And there, in the light of the morning sun, we saw what had struck Miss Bannister. It was—a batter pudding!

(Dramatic chord)

HENRY: It's still warm, Minnie.

MINNIE: Oh, thank heaven, I hate cold batter pudding.

HENRY: Come, dear little Minnie, I'll take you home—give you a hot bath—rub you down with anti-vapor rub—put a plaster on your back—give your little feet a mustard bath—then put you to bed.

SEAGOON: Do you know this woman?

HENRY: Devilish man!

MINNIE: Naughty Man!

HENRY: Naughty, naughty, horrible naughty man! Of course I do. This is Minnie Bannister, the world famous poker player. Give her a good poke and she'll play any tune you like.

SEAGOON: Well, get her off this cliff, it's dangerous. Meantime, I must report this to the Inspector. I'll call you later. Goodbye.

(Splash)

SEAGOON: As I swam ashore I dried myself to save time. That night I lay awake in my air-conditioned dustbin, thinking: now who on earth would want to strike another with a batter pudding? Obviously, it wouldn't happen again, so I fell asleep. Nothing much happened that night, except that I was struck with a batter pudding.

MILLIGAN: It's all rather confusing, really.

GREENSLADE: In the months to come, thirty-eight batter puddings were hurled at Miss Bannister.

MINNIE: Oooh!

GREENSLADE: A mad man was at large. Scotland Yard was called in.

(Short bridge)

HERCULES: Inspector Seagoon, my name is Hercules Grytpype-Thynne, special investigation. This batter pudding hurler…?

SEAGOON: Yes?

HERCULES: He's made a fool of the police.

SEAGOON: I disagree. We were fools before he came along.

HERCULES: You silly, twisted boy. Never the less, he's got to be stopped. Now, Seagoon…

SEAGOON: Yes, yes, yes, yes, yes?

HERCULES: Please don't do that. Now, these batter puddings, they were obviously thrown by hand?

SEAGOON: Not necessarily, some people are pretty clever with their feet.

HERCULES: For instance?

SEAGOON: Tin Cringingknut.

HERCULES: Who's he?

SEAGOON: He's a man who's pretty clever with his feet.

HERCULES: What's his name?

SEAGOON: Jim Flatcrock.

****

What more can I say?

ACT II: THE BRITISH HAVE COME

It seems appropriate, in order to make a smooth segue from the BBC to the U. S. A., to hear from someone who was born in England, but who worked for most of his career in North America. The party in question was given the name Angus Young at birth and later changed it to a more familiar *nom de plume*.

He was a versatile actor who did more comedy than any other genre, but he was more than able to handle anything that came his way.

Several of the people featured in one or another of these volumes were foreign born, but nearly all of them ended their productive lives in California. Andre Baruch was born in Paris, Les Tremayne in Balham, England, John Houseman in Bucharest, George Fenneman in Beijing, China, Max Geldray in Amsterdam, and the featured player in this act, now known as Alan Young, in North Shields at the far northern end of England close to the Scottish border

I spoke with Alan on March 31, 1987. Here is part of the result of that lengthy conversation.

****

JASON: Alan, you're originally from Northumberland, way up in the northernmost part of England, in North Shields.

ALAN: It's almost in Scotland, where I was born. If you're a penguin it's lovely country.

JASON: But you began your radio career in Canada. How did that all come about?

ALAN: My father was Scottish and like many Scots people, they like to leave the land of rocks, and cold, and snow, and the MacPhersons, and MacDonalds. He sailed to Canada and landed on the rocky shores with all the MacPhersons and MacDonalds. They just seem to want to travel and be with their own somewhere else, so we landed in Vancouver, British Columbia, or rather, Alaska first and then down to Vancouver where I got into radio.

JASON: Did you ever live in Saskatchewan? You used the town Ambleside, Saskatchewan on some of your radio shows.

ALAN: I didn't want to identify any real place. Ambleside is the Scottish name of a town in England. There is also one by that name in British Columbia, but I didn't want to make it Ambleside, British Columbia, so I made it Ambleside, Saskatchewan. Nobody would know what I was talking about that way.

JASON: I know that you got your better-known experience in Toronto, but obviously, you did more before that. You just said you started in Vancouver.

ALAN: I started at thirteen years of age in Vancouver doing radio shows, and I had my own show when I was seventeen, called *Stag Party*, not at all what that sounds like. It was carried across the Canadian Network and into what they called the Blue Network in the old days in America—in about four different towns, small towns. Then I went to Toronto where I did a sponsored show for the first time. From there, Eddie Cantor brought me to

New York. I had a return ticket to Canada, because I loved Canada, wanted to go back some time, but I cashed it in finally, never went back. I just stayed in America.

JASON: So you did a summer replacement for Eddie Cantor, and I believe it was that same fall that you got your own show as a regular feature.

ALAN: The sponsor put my show on along with another English performer named Gracie Fields. She had her own show for that winter and then she went back to England. I stayed on in America and just carried on with my little show.

JASON: There were many people on your various shows that we all know. One that immediately comes to mind is Jim Backus as Hubert Updike III.

ALAN: It's funny, I used to write part of the show and we needed a character actor. I would sit with the other writers, finally I said, "Look, you guys come up with a character. He must be the exact opposite of me. He must be brusque. He must be egotistical. He must be boastful, all of those things." So they came up with Hubert Updike III, the richest man in the world. I certainly was the poorest. The first person we got to read it was a young man named Arnold Stang, whom you may remember. He had no chin and was totally the wrong voice for the character. The first time we did it, it bombed. Then I remembered that Jim Backus had been auditioning a character for us as a fish peddler, which was an incongruous concept, but very funny. We blended his voice with our character, and he became Hubert Updike III, the richest man in the world.

Jason: But you did use Arnold Stang on your show.

Alan: We used him as other characters.

Jason: Ambrose?

Alan: That serves me right. We had a lot of people. I met Art Carney about five years ago at a party, and I called him Mr. Carney. He said, "Alan, don't you remember? I was a stooge on your radio show in 1945." I'd forgotten because we had many people like that on those shows. They were all new names to me. I'd just come fresh from Canada. Ed Begley played my girlfriend's father for about two years in New York. When we came out here he stayed in New York.

Jason: There was a character called David Dittenfeffer. Was that Walter Tetley? It certainly sounded like him.

Alan: No, it wasn't. David was played by a very young fellow, but I'm afraid I've forgotten his name. He was that age, just a young kid, but very, very studious, very studied. He just performed his role the way he should. He became a dancer, a very good dancer, ballet dancer. Then he married and settled down with kids and got out of the business.

Jason: Got into legitimate work?

Alan: Yep, he went straight.

Jason: You had Hal March on your show as a semi-regular.

Alan: Yes, when we got out to California we had Hal March. It was marvelous coming to California because my sponsor gave me an awful lot of money to hire guest stars. We had Edward G. Robinson, Rita Hayworth, Charles Laughton, all the big stars. I kept the records for years and years. Finally, I said to my wife, "We've got to get rid of some of those old recordings. Throw the small box out. They're too heavy." We gave the small box to the Goodwill. It contained all those lovely records, so I guess they're gone.

JASON: That's a shame.

ALAN: I could kick myself now, but who knew then. It was sad. I never had any photographs taken. I worked with Al Jolson, with Eddie Cantor, with Jimmy Durante, and many others, but I never had any photographs taken because I thought, "Oh well, I'll see them tomorrow." Tomorrow never came. I tell my kids now, "Get photographs taken with everyone you work with, because some day you'll really appreciate looking back." It's also something to leave to the library.

JASON: You had a couple of announcers who were certainly noteworthy. Kenny Delmar was with you for a while.

ALAN: That's an interesting thing. I brought a couple of characters down from Canada. Parker Fennelly did an old man for me. Then the writers created a man called Counselor Cartenbranch, which Kenny did. Our sponsor couldn't stand those two. We had to take them off. Fred Allen called up our manager and asked if we planned to use those two characters anymore. The manager told him we couldn't do it. Fred said he'd take them. He wrote them into big stars.

JASON: "Allen's Alley?"

ALAN: Right. Kenny was Senator Clagghorn and Parker was Titus Moody. I must say, Fred really did something with them.

JASON: That was quite a routine for many years.

ALAN: Marvelous. It was a great thing for Kenny. He was a good performer. He never really wanted to be an announcer. He wanted to be an actor.

JASON: He was later copied into a cartoon character, Foghorn Leghorn. Mel Blanc did the voice. I have a picture in front of me from your first television show in 1950. You're standing with some dancers, Jan Haller, Tom Mahoney, Jerry Antis and Jean Mahoney.

ALAN: That was the first chorus line in Hollywood.

JASON: That must have been shortly after your radio show left the air.

ALAN: I was in the doldrums for a while. I went into vaudeville, or stage shows, where I met the Mahoney's. I traveled with Liberace. We were a kind of a kids show in those days. When I came back to Hollywood, someone said, "Would you like to audition for this new thing, television?" Ed Wynn had a regular show on TV at that time. He was very big. He was most kind to me. He sat me down and told me all about television. In fact, he gave me one of his writers, Leo Solomon. Leo and Dave Schwartz and I wrote the first television show. The Mahoney's were the first dance line. I think we paid them $25, and they had to bring their own costumes. It

	was a hit, so we made it from there.
JASON:	Speaking of writers, let me backtrack a bit…back to your radio show. You had some soon to be, big name writers in that show. You had Jay Somers and Norm Paul, just to mention a couple of them. Norm was with George and Gracie for years.
ALAN:	Oh, yes, and there were some others who made it big. One of them is the head of the Writers Guild now and has done tremendously well. We had some awfully good writers.
JASON:	Stan Packard was another.
ALAN:	And, oh gosh, a couple of Jack Benny writers that came over and helped out in their spare time. They never wrote for me on television, because they were radio writers, then they moved on to movies.
JASON:	Between when you did your first *Alan Young TV Show*, and the one that we all remember, *Mr. Ed*, which we'll get to a bit later, apparently you were back in England for a while with the BBC.
ALAN:	Yes, television, for me, held nothing. Comedy went down the drain. Westerns came in and quiz shows. So I thought, I'm not going to sit around here waiting. I packed up my family and moved back to England. I worked for a company called Granada TV. They had just started up in January or February. I got there in April and we put on their first variety show. It was lots of fun. We stayed there for two years.
JASON:	That was about 1958 through 1960.
ALAN:	Exactly, thank you.

JASON: That would also have been about the time that *The Goon Show* began its last live run. I'm sure you remember *The Goon Show*.

ALAN: Of course. I'd go down to the radio studio and watch it. Peter Sellers was a dear friend of mine. We did a picture together, *Tom Thumb*. I'd go down and watch *The Goon Show* and frankly, I couldn't understand it even though I was English. I knew it was funny, but I couldn't figure out what they were talking about. They were a crazy, lovely bunch. It was very inside. I never did it, but I know it was fun to do. I came back to America just to reinstate my passport because if you stay out of the country in the country of your birth for more than three years you have to lose your citizenship. I had become an American citizen by then. So, I came back to New York to renew my passport, and I bumped into an agent who said, "Hey, George Burns has been looking for you. He says Alan Young is the only person a horse could talk to." He had made a pilot of a thing called *Mr. Ed*, and it didn't sell. He said the concept was all wrong. If he'd known that, he would have been in on the writing. He had a very homely horse, but he needed a beautiful horse. So when this was put together by Al Simon, who is a brilliant producer, George said, "That's the show!" We sold it without the pilot.

JASON: Before we get into *Mr. Ed*, let me go back briefly to the BBC. It was quite different working for the BBC, I would imagine, because while it's a private company it also operates under a Royal Charter, not a completely open corporation.

ALAN: I worked mostly for Granada which is ITV, (Independent television). I did some work for the BBC on some radio shows and, of course, I also worked for the CBC in Canada, which is the same network, but very different. I went to them one time for a raise. I was writing this half hour show, starring on it, directing it and getting $50 a week, which wasn't bad in those days, but wasn't enough for all that. I went to what they called the regional director. His vast experience in show business was that he'd been the principal of a boy's school. That, of course, gave him great knowledge of show business. I said, "I'd like to get $60 a week for writing, directing, and all that." He said, "But my dear chap, you'd be getting more than our concert violinist." I thought, "What the heck does that have to do with it?" Anyway, that's how they think. Concert violinists and poetry reading were much more important than a variety show. I know we were replaced once by a man who read poetry. One of his opening poems was *Secrets the Yellow Jonquil has Told Me*. I fell off my chair. I'd been put off for a yellow jonquil. That's the way it went.

JASON: There was really some strange programming on the BBC. I lived in Holland for several years, and I used to pick up the BBC on the radio; also Radio Luxembourg, another English speaking outlet. Radio Luxembourg was much more liberal. Did you ever work in any of the studios I'm familiar with, like Routen House or Paris Cinema?

ALAN: The only radio show I did in England was for the BBC. We did it in one of the big halls in London. It was for the British Empire Players, or something like that. I never worked in a studio, except to do promos.

JASON: What about your television show? Was that done in a theatre?

ALAN: Yes, we did those all at Hackney Empire, Woodgreen Empire, or some from Manchester, or the big theatre in Chelsea. Granada owned it.

JASON: So you were moving around the country? It wasn't all from London?

ALAN: We did about two from Manchester because of another funny arrangement they had. Granada bought the north, yet they were stationed in London. Any program they put together had to travel all the way to Manchester to broadcast, so it could truthfully be said it was coming from the north. A very peculiar way of doing things, but that's the way it was done. I said, "I can't get actors in Manchester. I don't want to play in Manchester." So they piped us in from Hackney Empire to Manchester and then released it from Manchester, as if it was coming from the north. I had the privilege of working in a theatre that had gas lights. That was the Woodgreen Theatre in London.

JASON: They still had them in the fifties?

ALAN: That was fifty-nine.

JASON: It's interesting that they still had gas lights at that time.

ALAN: Just in the dressing rooms and the hallways. On the stage they had regular television lighting, but they still had the gas jets, just in case. The English are always ready. They didn't put zippers in their flies for years and years because buttons were very reliable.

JASON: The British are very cautious and careful people, but, at the same time, delightful people.

ALAN: I think so.

JASON: Let's talk about *Mr. Ed*, since we've already touched on it. You had some really great people on that show. Do you want to start?

ALAN: You have a better memory than I. Go ahead. I know we had Mae West on one of them.

JASON: That, I didn't know.

ALAN: It was her first television show. Her only television show, I think.

JASON: That's interesting in itself. She was banned from the media after she did the "Adam and Eve" sketch on the *Charlie McCarthy Show*.

ALAN: Oh, that's right. Well, I don't know how she got on our show, but she was on it. I must say, CBS was down there with their censors at ready, because she was quite well known to ad-lib, but she was very good.

JASON: Sometimes the censors have no sense of humor.

ALAN: They also figured she was working with a horse, and anything you say to a horse *double entendre* has got to be kind of innocent, because nobody wants a horse to come up and see them sometime.

JASON: You had some regulars in that cast, people that we've seen on other shows. Larry Keating was your next-door neighbor.

ALAN: One of the best actors I've ever worked with in my life. He was just marvelous.

JASON:	He was one of the Harry Morton's on the *Burns and Allen Show* as well. Now we're talking about two shows coming from the same place.
ALAN:	That's how we got Larry. He'd just finished working with George Burns. George actually staged the first year of *Mr. Ed*. He wanted to make sure it got off to a good start. He would stage them and then have Arthur Lubin direct them for the camera. It was kind of rough because George would deliver his lines holding that cigar. He'd say, "Alan, do it this way." Finally I said, "George, I don't smoke." He said, "What's that got to do with it?" I said, "When you have a cigar in your hand and take a puff between lines it's very funny, but I can't do it that way." Finally, he caught on.
JASON:	He used to time his jokes with that cigar.
ALAN:	Also, when you're working with a horse, you don't dare raise your hands because the horse is going to follow the movement. Anything that's moving, he will follow. I had to stand there and just move my head. That, George couldn't get for a while. The cigar would get in the horse's face. Smoke would get in his eyes. We had some lovely problems. We ironed them out, but George staged the first thirteen weeks of the show.
JASON:	Did they use something on Ed to make him curl his lip the way he always did? I've heard they used honey.
ALAN:	Remember when you were a kid and you'd get peanut butter under your lip and try to get rid of it? That was what the trainer did to get the horse to talk. How he did it and how he got him to stop, was the real trick. I'm not at liberty to talk about

that because we're planning a two hour special of *Mr. Ed*, and I would be giving secrets away.

JASON: The outtakes from that show must have been hilarious.

ALAN: We never kept the mistakes. Arthur Lubin was very secretive about that. He said, "I don't want anything going out of here that shows that it isn't actually the horse talking." We had some funny bloopers where the horse would use a profanity because he missed something so all you saw on the screen was Ed swearing, which he would never do. He threw all the out takes away.

JASON: It was Allan Lane who did Ed's voice. I'm not at all familiar with him.

ALAN: Right, Allan 'Rocky' Lane. He was a star in 'B' westerns for years. I wasn't familiar with him either because I never saw any 'B' westerns.

JASON: So, he went from being a cowboy to being a horse.

ALAN: At first he didn't want to do it. He said, "I don't want to be the voice of a horse. Please don't mention my name in the billing." The first screen credits came out and they said that Mr. Ed was played by himself. Of course, the children thought that he really talked. Then the show was a hit and Rocky said, "Look, I'd like to get credit for this." Al Simon said, "No, sorry Rocky, we're getting too much mail about the horse doing his own voice. You signed a contract. That's it!" So Rocky never got credit for doing it on the screen, but he got enough money.

JASON: Was Mr. Ed a friend of Donald O'Connor's old side kick, Francis the mule, who also talked?

ALAN: Actually, *Mr. Ed* predated *Francis the Talking Mule*. They were stories from the old *Liberty Magazine*, from somewhere around 1933. Arthur Lubin owned them both. He owned *Ed* and he owned *Francis*. He sold *Francis* to Universal and kept *Mr. Ed* for what he thought television would be when it arrived. He certainly was right.

JASON: It ran for six or seven years.

ALAN: Six seasons.

JASON: Another guy who was on that show, who played a psychiatrist, was a man that everyone recognizes, although, they don't always pick up on his name, Richard Deacon, a tremendous character actor.

ALAN: He was on a lot of our shows. We used to get calls from a lot of stars saying, "I'd like to be on one of those little shows." Our director and producer were quite jealous about the show and usually said that they wouldn't quite fit. They'd be very graciously turned down.

JASON: The people who were regulars seem to fit a sort of a mold. Leon Ames was another regular.

ALAN: He took Larry Keating's place.

JASON: And Jack Albertson.

ALAN: When Larry passed away so quickly, we didn't know what to do. Jack came in as the brother of Edna Skinner. He played on quite a few shows until he left for *Chico and the Man*. Then we

	couldn't get him anymore. I look at some of those old shows now. I'm putting them together in a library—finally. I'm amazed at some of the small characters we had who are now big feature players.
JASON:	You once did a show on radio. I don't think there's any connection, but there was one radio show where you dreamed your uncle was a horse. Do you remember that?
ALAN:	Oh boy, no I don't.
JASON:	It was about 1945. I just thought it might ring a bell. The idea was somewhat similar.
ALAN:	No, not a bit. I'll be honest with you. I didn't like the radio show until we got to Hollywood. It was neither a variety show nor a situation comedy. The poor writers were trying to find out who I was, and I was trying to find out who I was, because I was used to being a variety performer. Situation comedy was very awkward for me, so I don't remember many of those shows too well until we got to Hollywood and got into a nice pattern. Then they began to make sense to me. Also, I had an accent. When I first got to New York a joke wouldn't go over, so I'd go to the writers and say, "You'd better change that joke." They'd say, "No, you're pronouncing it wrong. How do you say b-o-s-s?" I'd say, "Baass." They'd say, "No, its Baaws," because they were New Yorkers. I would come out with my back singed. I got very confused.
JASON:	Those shows were almost like variety shows. There was a lot of music for a thirty minute sit-com.
ALAN:	People like Jack Kirkwood were on it. He was a semi-regular.

JASON: Ken Christy?

ALAN: He played my father in law. He replaced Ed Begley. I did a screen test in New York, and they asked me to write it. So I wrote this little screen test, and I asked Ed if he would come in and play my father in law. He said he would, and he did it for nothing. Then I asked my leading lady at the time if she'd come in and do it. She said she didn't want to do a screen test. So we went down and shot it. Out of that screen test, Ed Begley got a contract to come to Hollywood, and I got a contract to come to Hollywood. My dear little leading lady was left wishing she had done it. Ed was terrific; such a good performer. I didn't realize what a good actor he was on the radio show because we didn't give him the good things to do until we got to Hollywood. Then we knew what an actor he was.

JASON: He finally did manage to win an Oscar.

ALAN: He certainly did, and his son is also doing well.

JASON: There were some other people on your first television show who are familiar to anyone who remembers radio, Joseph Kearns and Ben Wright.

ALAN: My director was a man called Alan Dinehart, Jr. He said, "Alan, we should get some faces on the television show." I said, "We can't afford it." He said, "I can get them." So he'd go down to the Masters Club and walk into the bar and say, "Who'd like to do television?" Well, sure! Two hundred and fifty bucks then, was very nice to have, so we had Alan Mowbray on all the time. William Frawley came on a great deal. It was through that that Bill got on the *I Love Lucy Show*.

Some marvelous character men and character women came.

JASON: Lucy had one of the first television shows, at about the same time as yours.

ALAN: It followed us. Lucy and Desi came down and saw how hard you had to work and how unsatisfactory early television was if you were a perfectionist, which she was. She said, "I want to do it on film." So they went on film. We had Billie Burke quite often and Cesar Romero about fifteen times.

JASON: *Burns and Allen* was shooting in the same building at the same time.

ALAN: They did the same thing. They went live for a while. They used the same studio we were using. Finally they said, "This is too much." So they went on film. I had a contract so I had to stay live.

JASON: Later, when you did shows on film, did you do them before a live audience or did you do them the way George and Gracie did? They shot them first and then showed them to a live audience to get their reactions.

ALAN: The review shows were done with a live audience. We had no tape. It was just on Kinescope.

JASON: And, of course, we both know those Kinescopes aren't worth much after a very short time.

ALAN: I have a basement full of them. They still work. I mean, you can still run them. The sprocket holes are good and everything, but they have no resale value.

JASON:	They don't have the kind of quality that can be used on the air.
ALAN:	Terrible! Terrible!
JASON:	It was an idea that had no future.
ALAN:	It was simply to keep a record. We used ours for rebroadcast in the east. That hurt the program. It was like looking through a snowstorm. It was all so primitive then. I remember doing a show once. We went on the air and I saw something flashing over the heads of the audience every now and then. The audience would look up and we would lose a laugh here and there. I found out later what was happening. We had a camera on an island in the middle of the house. Once a cameraman was out there he was stuck. It seems that his close-up lens went out on him. He spoke to the other cameraman on the intercom, and they figured out all of his shots. They'd throw the needed lens to where it was needed, across the audience and then toss it back after the required close-up. That's how primitive it was in those days.
JASON:	It might have been funnier if one of them had missed.
ALAN:	Certainly would have gotten some publicity.
JASON:	Those are the guys doing football now.
ALAN:	They were doing football then.
JASON:	When you look at old television reruns it's incredible what people would accept, but the concept was so new that they thought it was great, no matter what.

ALAN: People loved the mistakes. They loved to see something happen that wasn't supposed to. The only thing they didn't realize was what it was doing to the actor's heart. It was coming up through his mouth.

JASON: Bring us up to date. What are you doing these days?

ALAN: I'm very busy with voice-overs. I do voices for *The Smurfs*. I do voices for a new thing called *Duck Tales*. I've been doing *The Chipmunks* for years and also some stage work. I did four months in Vegas. Now we're planning a two hour *Mr. Ed* movie of the week which will be taking up most of my time. We have to be very careful because we don't have some of the people anymore.

JASON: That's very true. Looking down the list, some of the cast have passed on.

ALAN: Or, don't need to work, or just don't want to work anymore. But we still have our producer, Al Simon, and our director, Arthur Lubin, who are both very cultured in the medium. They're smart. I quit television after the Ed show and went to Broadway. Then I quit the business for eight years. I'd had enough. I'd been working since I was thirteen. But it's in your blood and you can't just stop. Connie Hines did. She got married and settled down. Leon is very happy at the beach, so we will have to create some other characters.

****

As of this date in 2014 Alan Young is still somewhat active in show business. He has had a long, long eight-decade career in the world of entertainment. Beginning in the early thirties at the

Orpheum Theatre on Granville Street in Vancouver and on CJOR radio, also in Vancouver, he has worked without a long sustained break for all of the years since. There were some lean periods, but Alan always managed to land on his feet.

He worked in every area of the performing arts at one time or another including a fine dramatic role in the movie version of *Time Machine* in 1960.

There were some near misses along the way. Just after signing a contract to do *Mr. Ed* he was asked to do the part of Barney Rubble on *The Flintstones*. He decided to turn it down because he thought it would have been a conflict of interest. In the end Barney was voiced by Mel Blanc.

Another 'close, but no cigar' situation developed when his agent informed him he had been accepted to begin a late night TV series. It did not happen. The show was hosted by another great performer named Steve Allen. Alan Young did, however, guest on Steve's show many times.

All things considered, this gentleman from the northern chill of England has done quite well for himself and those around him.

ACT III: BRIDGES UP!

A few radio shows came to us from Detroit, most notably, *The Lone Ranger* and *The Green Hornet*. Some from Cincinnati; remember *Ma Perkins*? There were also several broadcast from New York. *The Shadow* was one. San Francisco could lay claim to *One Man's Family*, among others. However, the lion's share of early programming originated from the hub of that era, Chicago. Many of them later relocated to California, but they were born and flourished in the windy city for a long time before that move.

The term, "Bridges Up" refers to the problems many Chicago actors experienced while trying to maintain their crowded schedules. Anyone worth his or her salt would be, at any given time, working at a variety of venues. The main studios were located in three buildings. Two of them, the Wrigley Building and the Tribune Tower, are nearly across the street from each other, but the third, the Merchandise Mart, is over a mile away. To complicate matters, as anyone familiar with Chicago knows, the Chicago River cuts through the downtown area, just north of the section called "The Loop." While the main studios were all north of the river, there were others scattered about on the other side, as was most of the shopping. Each north and south street has a bridge that would be raised for a considerable period of time every time a sizable ship or boat made its passage through the channel. In those days, there was much more river traffic than there is today. That meant that anyone who needed to cross over for any reason stood a good chance of getting trapped on the wrong side while the clock worked against him or her.

For this or any other imagined reason, the first thing they would say, somewhat sheepishly, was, "Sorry, the bridge was up."

It is time to hear from a few of those radio pioneers who began their lengthy careers as members of the "Bridges Up Club," in the mighty Midwestern metropolis called Chicago.

ACT III:
SCENE ONE:
THROCKMORTON
THE SECOND

Some of the early radio giants, who got their start in Chicago, came from other regions around the country and some from beyond our national borders, but many were native Midwesterners. One of those locals is the subject of this scene. Interestingly enough, he was born in the city from which my show, *Life in the Past Lane* was broadcast. He will tell us about that connection.

His name was Willard Waterman. We spoke on August 17, 1986.

****

JASON: You were born here in Madison, Wisconsin, but it's been a long time since you left here. Tell us a little about your history here.

WILLARD: It's been a long time since I was on your station, WIBA. I was on WIBA regularly when I was a freshman and sophomore at Central High. I worked with a trio. We did a morning hymn sing program and I read poetry from seven to seven-thirty every morning. Then I would walk over to Central High and spend the day in school. I lived out on Gilson Street. I went to Franklin Grade School and then Central High for the first two years. Then West High was built, so I transferred as a junior and I graduated from West High. I used to walk from my home on Gilson near Monona Bay over to West High and then back home after basketball practice. I then attended the University of Wisconsin until my junior year. I was kicked out. Dean Goodnight called me in and said, "Willard, I've watched you in the theatre at Bascomb Hall and I've heard you on WHA, our radio station. You seem to know what you're doing. It's probably a good thing because we do have a regulation that says you have to attend classes, but you don't seem to be able to find the time to do that. I think you'd better get out and try to make a living as an actor." So, I left and went to Chicago and started working there in the heyday of the soap opera and children's shows. I was there from 1934 until I came to L.A. in 1946.

JASON: Let me backtrack a little. When you worked at this station so long ago, was that in the old Tenney Building studios?

WILLARD: Yes, it was just off the square on one of the side streets.

JASON: At a time when we had music and dramatic studios. That was a whole different era.

WILLARD: I also did some radio drama out in Poynette. I used to drive out in an old Franklin car that I had at the time. We did radio dramas based on purloined detective scripts that had been sent in.

JASON: You mentioned that you did soaps when you went to Chicago. You were really busy with them at one time. I believe you were playing as many as forty roles a week.

WILLARD: When the soaps got started they were on all day in that area and the children's shows began in the late afternoon. I'd start in the studio, rehearsing, at seven or seven-fifteen in the morning and go right through the day and through the evening shows, which were *First Nighter, Grand Hotel* and *Fifth Row Center.* As you said, I would average about forty shows a week. There were no holidays in radio in those days. It was a very busy time, a very good time, I enjoyed it.

JASON: Did you ever get confused about which character you were doing? I have a case in my records, but I don't know how true it is. They say that you played two characters with the same name on two different shows, a couple of years apart. You were John Murray on *Lonely Women* and also on *Today's Children.*

WILLARD: That's right. There was some time in between. As a matter of fact, on *The Guiding Light*, I also played John Murray, from the West Coast, when the show moved to Los Angeles. I was with Betty Lou Gerson on *Guiding Light.* Erna Phillips, who wrote that show, used the same character names.

JASON: She wrote all three of those shows, and I think they were all Carl Webster productions if I'm not mistaken.

WILLARD: Absolutely correct.

JASON: Wasn't Mercedes McCambridge on *Guiding Light* with you, or was that a different time?

WILLARD: Mercedes was. It was the later years of the show when I was on it. She did a lot of soaps and many evening shows.

JASON: You also worked with Virginia Payne on *Ma Perkins* and several other soaps.

WILLARD: I was on *Ma Perkins* a few times but not as much as other shows. In those days we were all a kind of family around the Wrigley building where CBS was and the Tribune Tower where MBS (Mutual) was, and NBC was over in the Merchandise Mart. Working the three studios, we all saw each other almost every day. I'm sure I saw Virginia practically every day. I didn't have a regular character on *Ma Perkins* like I did on many other shows.

JASON: You worked with her on *Lonely Women* and *Today's Children*, too.

WILLARD: *Ma Perkins* was her regular show, but she did spots on those others.

JASON: She did *Ma Perkins* forever.

WILLARD: She was one of the first and one of the last. Before I got to Chicago *Ma Perkins* was on from Cincinnati. It moved to Chicago after I got there. Many of the people who did it in Cincinnati came with it to Chicago.

JASON: I was talking with Vincent Price a few weeks ago. He said that he did several soap operas anonymously. Did you ever use any other names than your own?

WILLARD: No, in those days we were all anonymous. There was no billing until later in the game, quite a bit later. Then AFRA (American Federation of Radio Artists) was created, and we got some billing. Until then people would write to your character name if they were writing fan mail or comments. Nobody knew what your name really was.

JASON: That was the only way they could do it then.

Looking through the casts of some of those early shows is like reading a Who's Who of radio, people like Olan Soulé and Raymond Edward Johnson. Marvin Miller was on just about everything at one time or another.

WILLARD: He had the longest list in the books. All of those people remained on radio for many years. There's an organization in Los Angeles called the PPB, (Pacific Pioneer Broadcasters.) I joined in 1965 or '66. The prerequisite was that you had to have worked in radio for twenty years to be eligible for membership. At the time, I was more than eligible because I had worked for nearly thirty years. It's wonderful to see all those people you've known for so many years in so many different places. In the early days, Chicago was the beachhead of radio where most of the shows originated. Then just prior to '46 when I moved to the West Coast, radio disappeared from Chicago. It went either East or West. Many of the people I knew in Chicago went to New York and many more came out here to California. As I said, we were really a family, and we like to remain in contact with each other. You brought up Vincent Price. I think most of his radio work was either in New York or on the West Coast. To the best of my knowledge he wasn't in Chicago at any time.

JASON: That's true. Of all the people I've spoken with so far you are the first who had so much background in Chicago. As you said, that's where it all began. Since I brought up Olan Soulé, I should also mention Barbara Luddy, his co-star on *First Nighter*. You were on that show for a long, long time.

WILLARD: I did almost all of the *First Nighter* shows in Chicago. When I moved to the West Coast I didn't do any because I was doing another show under exclusive contract. I hold a kind of record for most appearances on First Nighter. In the Christmas show, which they used to do every year, I played every character in it, except Mary. Mary was the only female on the show. Barbara Luddy played her. I played every other role at some time or another over the years they did it.

Jason: Here is a portion of the 1942 edition of that show. It was called "Little Town of Bethlehem" and on this version you played Cornius.

****

Cornius: Who is next and what is your name?

Joseph: Joseph, son of Jacob, son of Methan—

Cornius: Hold! Hold! Must everyone who registers recite his lineage to me? Did you not hear me say all I want is your name?

Joseph: But I am descended from the kings of Judea, from the great king David.

Cornius: I know. So is everyone in Bethlehem. The Roman emperor cares nothing about that. This is a Roman census.

Joseph: I'm sorry.

Cornius: Is this your wife?

Mary: My name is Mary. I too am of the line of David.

Cornius: Your voice sounds tired. Have you come far?

MARY: From the town of Nazareth in Galilee.

CORNIUS: Sit down on that bench and rest a while.

MARY: Thank you.

CORNIUS: Now, Joseph, what is your trade, how many children, what property?

JOSEPH: I am a carpenter. I have no property except my tools and the animal on which my wife has ridden from Nazareth. There are no children as yet.

CORNIUS: Very well, that is all.

JOSEPH: Pardon my lord, but we have no place to sleep. There was no room at the inn. Can you help me?

CORNIUS: This town is filled with those who have returned for the enrollment. I can do nothing. See that man talking to a soldier? That's Simon, a rich merchant. He has a large house. He may have room for you.

JOSEPH: Thank you.

****

JASON: During your years on *First Nighter* were you with Les Tremayne or Olan Soulé?

WILLARD: With Les and with Olan.

JASON: Do you go back as far as Don Ameche?

WILLARD: Yes, I did a few with Don, but he left not long after I got to Chicago. He left to go to Hollywood with a picture contract. I did both *First Nighter* and *Grand Hotel* with Don, at NBC in Chicago.

JASON: His background in Chicago was huge. He was also born in this area, in Kenosha, Wisconsin.

WILLARD: Absolutely. I told you about PPB. Last spring I was on a twentieth anniversary celebration of the PPB, and Don was there. He was on the dais with Les, Olan, and Lurene Tuttle, who died recently, so many of the old people who had been members since it first began.

JASON: Another name from *First Nighter*, one of the hosts, who was also one of *The Shadow* portrayers, was Bret Morrison.

WILLARD: Ed Prentiss was also a host at one time. Bobby Jellison was the page boy—*Smoking downstairs and in the outer lobby only*. Ed is on the west coast now. After he finished *Captain Midnight*, he came out here.

JASON: You just brought up *Captain Midnight*. A very good friend of mine, who passed away a year or so ago, used to play that role for some time. Do you remember Paul Barnes?

WILLARD: Oh, yes, he played it after Ed.

JASON: Everybody was interchangeable in those days. Since we're on the subject of kids shows, let's talk a little about *Tom Mix*. I have five different books that all have the same misinformation. They all say that both you and Hal Peary played Sheriff Mike Shaw on that program. I know from our discussion a couple of nights ago that, that is a fabrication.

WILLARD: I don't know how that got in there and remained in there in second editions. Hal and I both worked the show and as I told you, I played a character called Diamonds, who was a villain, a heavy as they call it, and also an old friend of Tom's called Longbow Billy. Hal did a character called Hot Barret, but neither of us ever played Mike Shaw. That was always Leo Curley.

JASON: There are so many different books. I get the feeling that people don't always do good research. They just take hearsay and pass it along as gospel.

WILLARD: I think that's true. I've seen almost all of those books. They all give credit to people who have given them information. I think some of the confusion is because of the three locations, Chicago, New York and Los Angeles. People whom they have interviewed were maybe New York people and didn't have much information about Chicago or Los Angeles, or *vice versa*. That has something to do with it.

JASON: When I was growing up in Chicago there was a musical show on Saturday evenings that I never missed, the *Chicago Theatre of the Air.* You had a dramatic part on it. Did you ever do any of the singing? I know you're a singer as well.

WILLARD: I'm not much of a singer. Most of the singers were opera people, Marian Weber and a lot of tenors from the Metropolitan in New York came on to do the singing roles.

JASON: James Melton, Richard Tucker, Jan Peerce and people like that. They also had a regular resident cast; Bruce Foote and Ruth Slater were two that I remember.

WILLARD: There were a lot of good singers in Chicago. There was a dramatic cast and a singing cast. The show was written that way so that the story was carried along by the dramatic cast and the arias were added by the singing cast. Bret Morrison did many of those. Marvin Miller, as well, and I did many of them, along with Betty Lou Gerson and almost all of the people in the Chicago group. They all did that show at one time or another.

JASON: In forty-five, you started on a comedy series that went from New York to Chicago to Hollywood in just a few years, *Those Websters*. It was a family that lived at 46 River Road in Spring City. A couple of people who worked with you, probably on the West Coast, were Parley Baer and—

WILLARD: Most of the cast started with me in Chicago.

JASON: Clarence Hartzell and Bill Idleson from *Vic and Sade* were there.

WILLARD: Clarence played Uncle Fletcher on *Vic and Sade*. He played another uncle on *Those Websters*. Gil Stratton started it. He played the young Webster and there was a gal who used to work on *Tom Mix*, Jane Webb and also Connie Crowder. Then, after we came out to the coast in forty-six, we picked up a lot of west coast people like Parley and others who played character parts.

JASON: In forty-six you did an episode called "The Great Marty." Here is the first scene from that show with you playing George Webster.

****

GEORGE: Jane! Jane! Look at this. Guess who this is from?

JANE: George, what's the use of guessing? I hate this game.

GEORGE: Go on, guess. I'll give you a hint.—One of the old gang.

JANE: Not Willie?

GEORGE: Oh no, we'll never hear from him. He borrowed five bucks the day we graduated.

JANE: Well then, who is it, George? This is silly.

GEORGE: Blue and white, fight, fight! Sock'em in the eyes, yea!

JANE: Not—oh, George!

GEORGE: Yeah, Marty, the Great Marty.

JANE: I thought you said it was someone I liked.

GEORGE: Liked? You were engaged to him.

JANE: Didn't have to like him, did I? What's the Great Marty have to say in that letter?

GEORGE: Here, read it.

JANE: *Dear Georgie.*

GEORGE: Ha, ha, he always called me Georgie, great guy.

JANE: *How's the old pal, you stick in the mud.*

GEORGE: A great kidder, too.

JANE: *Listen pal, I just read the announcement*—how many N's in announcement?

GEORGE: Ann—two, ounce—three, ment—four.

JANE: I thought so, great speller too. *Of the twenty-fifth reunion of our old high school graduation class. So I says to myself, Marty, it's going to be worth the price of a railroad ticket to see what that bunch of hicks I went to school with look like after twenty-five years.*

GEORGE: Great sense of humor, hasn't he? That's Marty for you.

JANE: *Well, you know me, Georgie, anything for a laugh. Tell the gang I'll be there with bells on. Don't bother to have a band down at the station to meet me. I don't know which train I'll arrive on, so I'll just take a taxi straight out to your place. Be seeing you pal, Marty.*

GEORGE: Hey, that's great. Isn't he just the same?

JANE: (with disgust) Just great!

****

JASON: There's one other show I want to bring up before we move on to your big one, *The Great Gildersleeve*. I always enjoyed *The Halls of Ivy*, with Ronald Coleman and his wife Benita.

WILLARD: That was a great show. I enjoyed it tremendously.

JASON: But, here again, there is an error in most of the books, or else there was some kind of crossover. I was listening to some of those programs just the other night and, while the books list you as Mr. Merriweather, the voice I heard was definitely Gale Gordon.

WILLARD: He was on *Halls of Ivy* but I don't think he played Merriweather. That was my character. I suppose it could be. It would depend on when it was. After I started doing *Gildersleeve*, they continued *Ivy*. They may have recast my role.

JASON: Gale did play the role but only on later shows. Here is an example of one of the earlier shows with you doing John Merriweather and Ron as William Todhunter Hall and Benita as his wife, Victoria Hall.

****

JOHN: I do hope I'm not disturbing you.

WILLIAM: On the contrary, Mr. Merriweather. I was looking forward to seeing you. Is there trouble on the campus?

JOHN: No, no, there isn't. No doctor, I'm not the bearer of bad news, in fact, I'm not the bearer of news at all.

WILLIAM: Good, then we can relax; discuss life, love and the pursuit of happiness.

JOHN: The pursuit of happiness will do doctor. Life and love at my age are delicate subjects. To be honest, the real reason for my visit is your wife. I don't think I have to remind you what a fan of hers I am, always have been.

WILLIAM: I know, and as president of the Victoria Cromwell Hall fan club, I welcome you as a member.

JOHN: I'll attend every meeting doctor. I'm afraid I got a little carried away last week. You know what a hobbyist I am, always fooling around with gadgets, electric trains, and stuff. I went to work at such an early age, I'm now having my second childhood, I guess. Don't be surprised if I show up sometime wearing a Hopalong Cassidy suit and swinging a yo-yo.

WILLIAM: You'd be quite welcome wearing a pinafore Mr. Merriweather, but what's the point?

JOHN: Well, the point is, doctor, when I learned that Mrs. Hall was going to do a number in the Junior Follies I smuggled a recording machine into the auditorium.

WILLIAM: You did? What a splendid idea. Did you get her song?

JOHN: Every magnificent note of it, for posterity. It's much too good for them.

WILLIAM: I hope I can hear it sometime.

JOHN: I brought it with me.

WILLIAM: You did? That was thoughtful of you.

JOHN: Thanks, but in all honesty, I must admit it was also a matter of self-preservation.

WILLIAM: Mrs. Merriweather?

JOHN: Mrs. Merriweather!!

****

JASON: Is it true that sometimes when people were off a show for a couple of weeks for illness or whatever reason, someone else in the cast might play the role?

WILLARD: I guess it happened. They tried to avoid it as much as possible, but I suppose it probably happened that someone was incapacitated suddenly. They would have to use whoever was available.

JASON: I know it happened frequently on *The Lone Ranger*. They had definite problems with John Todd, who played Tonto.

WILLARD: *The Lone Ranger* was in Detroit, so a lot of people don't know much about it. They didn't have as large a selection of talent, so they had to make do. Once, while I was in Chicago, George Trendle came over with a big audition. What it actually was, they were trying to hold someone over Brace Beemer's head. I won the audition. They offered me a contract to go to Detroit and play lesser roles on the show with the idea that I could step in and play *The Lone Ranger* if they had trouble with Beemer's contract. I refused for two reasons. First, I didn't want to be held over Beemer's head and second, I could make much more money in Chicago than they offered me.

JASON: Brace Beemer was a strange person from what I've heard. He used to run around with a mask on, even before he was *The Lone Ranger*.

WILLARD: I understand that. There were some conversations about it.

JASON: I have pictures. Let's talk about *The Great Gildersleeve*. He was a character who got his start on *Fibber McGee & Molly* way back in 1937, played then by Hal Peary.

WILLARD: *The Great Gildersleeve* was the first spinoff. As you said, it came from the *Fibber* show and Hal did play him there. 1950 is when I took it over. That was the year, if you remember, that CBS was raiding all the NBC shows. They got Benny to come over, and Phil Harris and quite a few of the other shows. Hal's agent, who was William Morris at the time, sold him to CBS under contract, thinking they could deliver his show, but when it came time to do that, the sponsor, Kraft, did not want to change networks. They wanted to stay with NBC. So with Hal under contract to CBS, it became necessary for NBC to recast the part. When it came time to do that, Frank Pittman, who was the director and the agency rep, called me. It was well known at the time that Hal and I had a very similar quality. It was hard to tell our voices apart except that mine was a little deeper than his, but our quality was very much the same. So they called me and said, "Willard, we don't need you to audition to see if you can act, but we wonder if you can come in and read for John Elliotte, Andy White, and Paul West, the writers, and us, to see if it's reasonable to go with a sound-alike, or whether we should go with an entirely different voice. If you'd come in and read, it would also give you a chance to decide whether you want to do it." It was true that I had reservations about taking over a well-established character. So I went in and read it and the more I read it—the more I realized that the show was so well written by the boys, that it didn't take any effort to fit in. I just played the character the way it was written.

JASON: When I listen to tapes of *Gildersleeve*, I can only tell who-is-who by the date, especially with the aging of sound. Things change a little on tape as time goes by, but the resemblance is uncanny. Apparently, it wasn't something you had to work hard at.

WILLARD: No, I didn't work on it at all. As a matter of fact, just playing the character the way it was written pushed my quality a little bit higher so it did come out the same. For many weeks a lot of people didn't know there was a change.

JASON: I repeat—the only way to know is by the date.

WILLARD: Yes, that is the only way. Anything after 1950 was me and before 1950, was Hal. The show started in 1941 and when I took over in 1950, I played it until 1959. We each did nine years.

JASON: Here's a small sample from the annual Christmas show you did in 1951 on *The Great Gildersleeve*.

****

GILDY: Hello Paula.

PAULA: Come in. My, it's snowing out, isn't it?

GILDY: Just a little.

PAULA: Look at you. You have a big snowflake right on the end of your nose.

GILDY: I do? Well, cold nose, warm heart.

PAULA: Let me take your coat.

GILDY: Thank you. Beautiful tree Paula, and Christmas presents. Are all those for me?

PAULA: No, but you can help me finish wrapping them.

GILDY: Fine—lots of presents.

PAULA: Mother and I have lots of relatives, and I couldn't forget those darling children down at the hospital. There are five of them that Santa Claus may not remember.

GILDY: Good for you, Paula. It'd be a shame if any little kids were forgotten on Christmas.

PAULA: Put your finger on this ribbon while I tie the knot.

GILDY: All right. Interesting paper you're using Paula, mistletoe design.

PAULA: (laughing) Just put the package over there.

GILDY: I'll hold it over your head. You know what that means—mistletoe?

PAULA: Throckmorton! Aren't you rushing the season a little?

GILDY: Only three more shopping days.

PAULA: You'd better put the package down there by the tree.

GILDY: Shucks!

****

JASON: You mentioned another name that fits the history books, Frank Pittman. Wasn't he responsible for Fibber McGee's closet?

WILLARD: He may have begun it when he was a sound man, because that's how he started in the business. He may well have started the closet. That is something that really is a landmark of radio. Everybody knows McGee's Closet.

JASON: I remember well, seeing some of those shows in Chicago and watching the sound effects men work their magic. They were mostly what I watched.

WILLARD: That was a thing we actors used to think about a lot when we did those audience shows. Nobody watched the actors. They were all watching the sound men. It was good entertainment to see those guys pick up a couple of coconut shells and make the horses hooves in a western. For the closet bit—I think they used to use a big step ladder. They'd put a thing on each rung. Then knock them off a bit at a time. There was one little tinkling bell that always signaled the end of the effect.

JASON: There were some people on *Gildersleeve* that nearly everyone knows. One of them was Bea Benaderet, who died not long ago. Another was Dick Crenna.

WILLARD: Dick played Bronco, Marjorie's husband and Mary Lee Robb was Marjorie. Before her—it was Lurene Tuttle. Judge Hooker was Earle Ross. Nobody looked more like an old goat than he did. Peavy was Dick LeGrand, and the barber was Arthur Q. Bryan.

JASON: Arthur was a lot of things. He was the original Elmer Fudd. Another one was Walter Tetley, who was a veteran actor at a very young age.

WILLARD: He was. He started years ago on *The Children's Hour* doing an imitation of Sir Harry Lauder, singing and doing a Scottish dialect. He was the original Leroy on *Gildersleeve*, and he did *The Phil Harris Show*. He was all over the dial. There was no one in the world who could read comedy lines like him, juvenile comedy lines.

JASON: I remember hearing him with W. C. Fields on *Your Hit Parade.* They would have a comedy segment in between songs. You had another juvenile actor for a period of time, someone who also did David Nelson on *The Ozzie and Harriet Show* before David himself did the part. He was Tommy Bernard.

WILLARD: That's right. Your knowledge of these shows is fantastic. I know a lot of people who are students of old time radio. Sometimes I think that people who have made a study of old time radio know more about it than those of us who were there. We tend to forget a lot of things that went on. They have great collections of old tapes. That's another story, where those old tapes came from. Most of those old shows were done live. There was no recording. They made some records, what we called reference records. One thing that preserved most of them was the fact that, for each show we did, they made one of those big fifteen inch platters that were sent overseas to *Armed Forces Radio Service.* Nobody thought too much about it at the time, but that was the only recording that was made of most of them. What happened, I guess, was that when the discs came in, a lot of the armed forces engineers realized what kind of a bonanza they had, so they put all those fifteen inch records on tape. All of the sudden they began to appear on the market. Some of them made a few bucks out of it. The actors didn't make anything because there were no restrictions. As far as the union was concerned, those shows were all done live.

JASON: You did some *Great Gildersleeve* television that ran concurrently with the radio shows.

WILLARD: We did thirty-nine films for the television series, one year's production. That was all there were.

ACT III: SCENE ONE: THROCKMORTON THE SECOND

JASON: The TV show never did quite make it.

WILLARD: No it didn't, and there was a reason for that. The producer that NBC hired didn't know anything about the radio show. I don't know if he ever heard it. He had some kind of preconceived notion that Gildersleeve was a skirt chaser. It was very unlike Gildersleeve. He had an eye for the ladies, but if they turned around, he ran.

JASON: He was always running away from Eve Goodwin and Leila.

WILLARD: Leila and he were an item, but he never came close to getting married. Also, we weren't able to use Walter Tetley as Leroy and that was a damn shame.

JASON: Walter was quite a cut-up off mike, wasn't he?

WILLARD: Oh, yeah, he was a lot of fun. We had a ball in the studio doing the shows. Rehearsals were always lively. We never knew quite where Walter was going to be or what he was going to be doing.

JASON: I remember reading a story about him moving the studio clocks forward a couple of minutes, which, of course, created panic on radio.

WILLARD: That is panic. He did that one time. We supposedly started the show and everybody was using blue language. The producers were going crazy, but we knew it wasn't going over the air. There were many things that Walter did that were enjoyed by us, the cast.

JASON: Wouldn't it be great if we could get some dramatic radio back on the air so we could start using our imaginations again?

WILLARD: Yes, it would be wonderful if we could do that. There was no more satisfying thing than doing the radio shows that we did.

****

There was a big problem for the performers in those early days of radio. They got no credit for their work. They were strictly anonymous voices. Even more importantly, once a show was over, their financial rewards were also over. Royalties and residuals were non-existent. In 1937 part of that situation was corrected. Willard Waterman was one of a group of people who were instrumental in helping their fellow actors get what they richly deserved. He was a member of the founding group of AFRA (American Federation of Radio Artists), which later became AFTRA (American Federation of Television and Radio Artists). They fought hard for those missing rights. Today those fringes are respected.

Will was active for a time on the silver screen, while continuing to show up on television once in a while on shows like *77 Sunset Strip*, *F Troop*, and *The Dick Van Dyke Show.*

He left us in 1995 at the age of eighty. We will not forget his entertaining work.

ACT III:
SCENE TWO
RADIO IDOL

Near the top of the list for number of radio performances, this radio matinee idol was a very recognizable voice on the airwaves. He was doing an average of forty-five broadcasts a week at one point in his long career. It was not that unusual for talented radio actors to do multiple shows in those years, but forty- five was a big number. Altogether, he accounted for more than 30,000 appearances on mike.

He was a prime candidate for the "Bridges Up Club" in Chicago.

On March 14, 1987 I had a long discussion with Les Tremayne. Now you, too, will know what he had to say.

****

JASON: Les, I know you were born in London. Tell me how you came to be on Chicago radio.

LES: I started in motion pictures in England with my mother in 1916 during World War I. My father was an American. My mother was an actress. I was under the care of a tutor while I was in England. Then I came to the United States during the war. I don't know how it happened. All of the sudden we were pretty poor. I went to school on the great west side of Chicago, which was a pretty tough neighborhood. They heard me speak like a little English gentleman. The kids started hitting me on the nose and other places. That went on for about two or three months until I learned to fight dirty the way they did and lost most of my English accent. Then it wasn't fun for them anymore. I knocked around in show business in America. I did just about everything. I was a hoofer. I was in vaudeville for a while, and doing little theatres, and community theatres. You name it. I did everything I could get my hands on, just as everyone does when trying to get into show business. I've been in it now for seventy years. In 1930, I got into radio.

JASON: You started on soap operas. You did quite a few soaps.

LES: They weren't known as soaps in those days. They were called daytime serials. One of the first things I did was a thing called *Night Court*, which entailed knowing dialects, doing all sorts of characters, which we're not allowed to do anymore. The ethnic types don't like to be, they think, ridiculed. In doing that, in bringing everyone into using plain English, we lost a lot of color, unfortunately, and it restricted actor's performances to a great extent. I did all sorts of shows, little half hour dramas and kid's shows. I was *Secret Agent X-9*. I was *Flash Gordon*. I started in 1930, and for the first eight months I was in the business, I didn't get any sort of money at all. They just didn't pay in those days. The first money I did receive was about two and a half dollars for a show on WGN, which I think was called *Uncle Quinn's Scallywags*. That was Quinn Ryan's show. He was a big man there at the time. The first time I made some real money— don't forget, this was the depression—I made five dollars on one show and seven-fifty on another. I'd been trying to track down a young director named Blair Walliser who was at WGN. I finally caught up with him on the street one day and he said,

"Come along with me. I'm going up to the Drake Hotel." From the Tribune Tower we walked the mile or mile and a half to the Drake in the bitter cold. He put me on a show up there. It was one of the WGN contest shows. They were always having them. WGN stood for "World's Greatest Newspaper," which was the *Chicago Tribune.* That was their slogan. After I had done the five dollar show he said, "If you'd like to stick around, we're doing another one at nine o'clock tonight. That one will pay seven-fifty." Seven dollars and fifty cents, I stress. I was, as I said, pretty broke, just as everyone was in those days. I had no money, and I was a hungry, skinny kid. I said, "Yes, I'll stay." I sat in the Drake Hotel lobby until nine, from about twelve-thirty or one in the afternoon, pretty darn hungry. I finally did the show and got my twelve-fifty. From then on, I started on a roll. When a young lady named Ann Ashenhurst came out from New York to start looking for actors to play in a new soap opera called *The Romance of Helen Trent*, they picked me to become Helen Trent's first leading man, a man called Grant Douglas. I was with the show for several years. It started in 1934. Then things branched out from there.

JASON: You mentioned seven-fifty for a single show. Actually, that was pretty good in those years.

LES: It amounted to twelve-fifty for two shows.

JASON: But that wasn't too bad. I spoke with Gale Gordon, and he said he was getting three dollars a show and had to kick back ten per cent to the producer.

LES: Don't forget, my first show was two dollars and fifty cents.

JASON: Which is about what he was netting.

LES: That's about right.

JASON: You also mentioned the ethnic aspect. We know that Amos 'n' Andy was canceled for that reason, but there was another big show that met the same fate. It starred J. Carrol Naish. It was *Life with Luigi*.

LES: But that was later on.

JASON: Still, in its time, it was a very funny show. You worked with Ann and Frank Hummert on some soaps.

LES: Yes, in Chicago, they had a number of them.

JASON: *Betty and Bob* was one. *Helen Trent* was another.

LES: I was on *Betty and Bob* for five years. I was Coach Hardy on *Jack Armstrong, the All American Boy*. I did many shows that wouldn't even be remembered. I was on *Skippy* and *Ma Perkins, Chandu, the Magician,* and *The Kate Smith Show, Inner Sanctum,* and *Grand Central Station* and later on, some more prestigious shows, *The Chesterfield Supper Club* with Perry Como, *Kraft Music Hall* with Bing. I did *Kraft* with Edward Everett Horton. With my former wife, Alice Reinhardt, who played Chi-Chi, on *Life Can Be Beautiful*. Much, much later, in the fifties I was on *The Woman in My House*, which was a takeoff on *One Man's Family*.

JASON: Which you also did at one time.

LES: That's right. I was on *One Man's Family* on television. On radio, another beautiful show, *I Love a Mystery* out of New York.

JASON: In both cases, working with Carlton E. Morse.

LES: He is a good friend of mine. I was the host on *Hallmark Hall of Fame*. Things started to happen for me around 1935. I followed Don Ameche in five different parts on four different shows. He was playing Coach Hardy on *Armstrong* and Bob on *Betty and Bob*. When he left those shows I took them over. This was quite a big thing in Chicago because Don was THE leading man before I came along. When he went to Hollywood in thirty-six, I took over the leading man role on *Grand Hotel*, which was one of his shows. And then, when he left *First Nighter*, and it came back to Chicago—I became leading man on that, too. I was with *First Nighter* for about ten years altogether. I was on that show from 1933 until 1943—about the middle of forty-three.

JASON: Your co-star on *First Nighter* was always Barbara Luddy.

LES: Dear little Barbara Luddy. She was a beautiful actress with a sexy, gorgeous voice. She left us about ten years ago. She was a lovely girl, one of the finest actresses I ever worked with.

JASON: After you left the show, she worked with Olan Soulé until the end of the run.

LES: As I understand it, they auditioned and rotated four different people. One was Will Waterman, one was Ed Prentiss, I don't know who the third one was, then Olan. They finally decided to stay with Olan.

JASON: Willard worked on most of those shows for quite a few years.

LES: He worked on many of them. We had a compact little stock company on that show. We didn't restrict it to the people who worked it every week. We had to work fast. We only had two and a half hours of rehearsal for that show. That included the orchestra rehearsal. Playing to twenty-five million people every week, a half hour show, you had to be pretty quick. You had to know what you were doing. They couldn't really use too many new people who didn't know the format and the routine.

JASON: There were some great names that appeared on *First Nighter* consistently, people like Parley Baer and Marvin Miller.

LES: Marvin was Mr. First Nighter for a long time, the host of the show. So was Bret Morrison.

JASON: Michael Rye and Macdonald Carey.

LES: Mac Carey was our host for a long time back in Chicago before he went into pictures.

JASON: There was another one of your shows with a similar format called *Brownstone Theatre*.

LES: I was the leading man on that, out of New York.

JASON: You followed Jackson Beck.

LES: I don't know. Jackson is a friend of mine, but I don't know that he played that before I did. Here's an interesting story. The first dramatic show that this young lady did in New York was as one of my leading ladies. I had a different one each week. Her name was Jan Miner. She later became the Palmolive girl for some twenty years. Madge, I think it was, on the commercials, so little Jan has done very well.

JASON: How about Gertrude Warner, who was one of the Margo Lanes on *The Shadow*?

LES: By golly, you're bringing up names I've almost forgotten. Gertrude Warner was a fine actress and a lovely girl. She was very pretty. Yes, I worked with her.

JASON: How about a show that I don't know at all, but I found in one of my books—*The Jackie Gleason—Les Tremayne Show*.

LES: Bob Crosby and I had a show out here in Hollywood in 1943 and 44. It was called *The Old Gold Show*. When Bob left the show during the war—I think he went into the Marines. On a one week's notice they moved the show, and in those days you took a train from Hollywood to New York. We had to make the move within one week. In other words, we did the last show out here on a Sunday afternoon and opened the show in New York the next Sunday afternoon. We picked up a rough and tumble comedian named Jackie Gleason, who wasn't known at all outside of a few night clubs. They used him as a comedian on the show. I continued to do my stuff and Andy Russell was the singer who replaced Crosby.

JASON: There was another show that was one of my favorites while I was growing up on which you did dramatic parts. It was *The Chicago Theatre of the Air*. The thing I remember most about it was not the show itself. It was the commentaries by Colonel Robert

R. McCormick in the middle of each show when we'd all leave the room to get a snack or whatever.

LES: I worked it a few times. Marian Clare (Weber) was the girl singer. She was one of the Colonel's favorites. He built the show for her, along with her husband, Henry, who was the conductor of the orchestra, a fine musician.

JASON: There was a good friend of mine who appeared with you on the air. His name was Harry Elders. He did a lot of soaps.

LES: Harry was a fine guy. I was very fond of Harry. He was our 'call boy' for a while on *First Nighter*. You know, "*First curtain.*" "*Curtain going up.*" I think Harry did very well. As far as I know, the last I heard, he was still working in Chicago, but living in Colorado.

JASON: The last contact I had with him was doing some spots in Chicago when I had a recording studio there. He did a lot of training and industrial recordings.

LES: He was also president of AFTRA at one time, which incidentally, I helped to form.

JASON: Let's talk a little about *The Thin Man*. You worked for Himan Brown on that one, as well as some other shows. Again, you had the leading role as Nick Charles opposite Claudia Morgan, the only woman who ever played Nora. There was another name you wouldn't expect to hear on a detective format, Parker Fennelly.

LES: Oh yeah, Parker, bless him. I'm not sure how Parker is. I think he left us. I believe that's what

I've heard, but I'd rather not make it gospel because, although I am audio chairman for Pacific Pioneer Broadcasters, I'm not sure about Parker. He used to come in and play various parts on various shows. He used to play on *The Thin Man.* I was Nick Charles for four or five years in New York. Claudia, who is now gone, was a sweet gal, fun to work with. There were only two or three that I ever worked with who weren't fine people. It was a close-knit little group. I don't mean by that that we kept others out. People like to say we did. We practically lived together. We worked together all day long, every day of the week, Sundays, Holidays, even Christmas. It didn't make any difference. There was a time in Chicago when I did forty-five shows a week. For about three years I did that. I never stopped running. It was a very active life and a very satisfactory life. The radio was the greatest thing that ever happened for performers. It made us home owning, tax-paying, family-raising, stay in one place people who made a regular salary for the first time in show business history. You could have a triple 'A' credit rating, own everything you wanted. At least you weren't in debt most of the time. It brought with it a certain respect that actors had never had before. People don't like to give actors much respect, because they're afraid they'll get out of hand. It's no wonder, because they've been kicked around for centuries.

JASON: Radio gave the audience a chance to use their imaginations and gave the actors a chance to really act, because they had to create images in our minds.

LES: I'm glad to hear you say that. A lot of people say, "You don't act. You just stand there and read something," which is not true at all. You had to be a pretty fine actor in order to portray some of the things you did and, as you said, make the audience live it with you. You mentioned Hi Brown. Yes, I worked with him a number of times along with his brother, Mende. My former wife, Alice Reinhardt and I did the *Abbott Mysteries* series. We played the Abbotts. We also did a thing called *The Tremayne's*. That was a talk show out of New York. It was on for a year or so. We did everything on that show from reporting on The Fighting Lady coming into the harbor (the big aircraft carrier)—all the way to un-wrapping a two-thousand year old mummy from Peru at the American Museum of Natural History. I've photographed a lot of Mayan sites down in the Yucatan for Columbia University and UCLA where I studied archeology. I'm very much interested in archeology. I've done a lot of things. I was closely associated with Lincoln Borglum at one time. He was the man who sculpted Mount Rushmore. I had the pleasure of taking a jack-hammer up on Mount Rushmore, helping to chop off some of the rock. I co-owned a ranch with him out there. He died recently, too.

JASON: So many of the radio people have passed away within the last few years, many that you worked with. Julie Stevens died about a year ago. Is Virginia Payne still with us?

LES: No, Virginia died several years ago, and Ernie Chappell, who was married to Claudia Morgan. He was the voice of Pall Mall Cigarettes on one of those big mystery shows, *Big Story*, out of New York. There comes a time for all of us, I'm sorry to say, but it was great. I've been in TV since 1939. I started on W9XYZ, an experimental station in Chicago. I starred in three series on television. On *Ellery Queen*, I played his father. I did *One Man's Family* in New York and Hollywood, and *Shazzam*

ACT III: SCENE TWO: RADIO IDOL

for the kids. I did that about ten or twelve years ago. I was Mr. Mentor, the old guy who drove the truck, as the kids used to say.

JASON: You also worked on *Perry Mason.*

LES: Oh, yes, *Perry Mason, The Virginian, Alfred Hitchcock, Bonanza, Hunter, Video Theatre, Lux Radio Theatre, The Gray Ghost, The Rifleman, Red Skelton*, you name it. I've done about thirty or thirty-five motion pictures.

JASON: So many radio names were on early television.

LES: There was a great group of them. They were the best people around, so they did most of the work. They were facile. They were resilient. And, they were clever.

JASON: And, quick to travel from one studio to another.

LES: I'll say, gosh, I had doormen, cab drivers, actors holding open sound lock doors, everybody getting out of the way as I ran from one studio to another. Half of the time it was across town from the Merchandise Mart to the Wrigley Building in Chicago, from 52nd and Madison to NBC at 30 Rock in New York. You just never stopped running. Chicago was spread out all over the place. Radio stations everywhere. They were really spread out. The Merchandise Mart is at least a half-a-mile from the Wrigley Building, where NBC was. From WGN, trying to get across Michigan Boulevard to Mutual in a snow storm was something. We had a thing there called the "Bridges Up Club." Chicago, you know, is bisected by a river. Some of the stations were on one side of the river and some were on the other side. The "Bridges Up

Club," I think, is an apocryphal tale. They tell the story of how we hired a launch in the river so, that if a bridge was up and a boat was going through, we could jump in the launch and go around the boat, so we could get to the other side and do our shows. It's a nice story. I don't mess around with pictures anymore. After all, the business, in America at least, is geared to young people. They don't want old folks any more than they have to have them. If you happen to be a big star, you might get a part in a movie nowadays. For the most part, movies are a lost art for people my age.

JASON: Howard Duff made a comment to that effect on an earlier edition of *Life in the Past Lane*. He said at his age he gets all kinds of eccentric radical parts.

LES: That's about right. I starred in a thing called *Holy Wednesday*. The title was later changed to *Fangs*. It was the story of a dirty old goat, who lived down in a little Texas town of about five-hundred people. He was pretty eccentric. People didn't like him very much. If someone was nasty to him he killed him with rattlesnakes, put him in his car and shoved him off a cliff. Car and all went down the drain. You never saw the picture because the distributers put a hold on it. It's on a shelf somewhere.

JASON: Probably just as well.

LES: Probably! You've heard about *North by Northwest* and *The War of the Worlds*. I was one of three leads in *War of the Worlds* for George Pal.

JASON: And *Fortune Cookie* with Jack Lemmon.

LES: *Say One for Me* with Bing, *The Gallant Hours* with Jimmy Cagney, *It Grows on Trees* with Irene Dunne, *Francis Goes to West Point* with Donald O'Connor—it goes on and on.

****

Finally, in 1995, Les Tremayne was recognized by his peers for his massive contributions to his chosen field of endeavor. They elected him to the Radio Hall of Fame, where he richly deserves to be. Many of his performances are still available to be enjoyed by all of us.

In 2003 his heart gave out. He was ninety years old and had spent most of those years entertaining us. As you have read, he also entertained himself doing the work he loved.

The bridges in Chicago are still there of course, but they are no threat to an industry that, alas, no longer exists.

Act III: Scene Three
From Tents to Hollywood

Here we have another Midwesterner who found his niche on Chicago radio, but that is not where his performing career began. He was born in La Harpe, Illinois, not far from Burlington and Keokuk, Iowa. At a young age his family moved to Des Moines, where he spent his teen years. He was a man of small stature, but with a big voice, which made him perfect for the airwaves.

We have already heard a little about him from Will Waterman and Les Tremayne, but it is time for much more detail. His name was Olan Soulé. This discussion took place on February 21, 1987.

****

JASON: You told me something about your background that I wasn't aware of. You have a definite Wisconsin connection.

OLAN: Yes, definitely. My first contract in the business was what was called a junior equity contract. Junior equity meant that you had been in the business not over two years. I was in a tent show, the *Jack and Maude Brooks Tent Show* up in Wisconsin. That was the very beginning of my career back in 1926.

JASON: Tent shows were a little similar to vaudeville circuits, weren't they?

OLAN: Not really, Jason. Tent shows, and, of course, there were many of them, played the same territory for twenty-five or thirty years. This was before radio or television. I'm talking about over sixty years ago. You'd get up at six bells. You'd play Monday through Saturday and travel on Sundays. There were all small towns, very close together. We moved by truck and car. We'd do six three-act plays. Regular three-act plays, like those done in permanent stock. They did what they called specialties between acts—singing and dancing, things like what I did. Basically, it was a regular entertainment evening, a three-act play with vaudeville acts in between. I was a juvenile of course, only seventeen. I claimed to be twenty, but I was only seventeen. I did a full line of juvenile specialties between acts. I doubled on drums in the orchestra, was the prop man, worked on the setup and tear down of the tents, and drove the canvas truck. That was all for thirty bucks a week.

JASON: So, what did you do with your spare time?

OLAN: I slept. It was real exciting. It was good schooling for a young actor, if you were in a good company who did good bills, and we did. Jack Brooks, when he'd set up his program in the spring and the summer, would bring in a good director from Chicago, and he hired good people too, actors and actresses. So, it was really terrific schooling for me.

JASON: I assume you were doing one a day with that kind of format.

OLAN: We did a show in the evening, that's all, no matinees.

JASON: What brought you from tent shows to the world of radio?

OLAN: In about 1931, I decided New York was ready for me. I had done some stock in the meantime in St. Louis. I got married there in 1929. Then I got another tent show in Kentucky and Tennessee. We left a good job there, my wife and I. She wasn't in the business. We went to New York. I didn't realize how many theatre guild people were out of work, so I couldn't even get looked at for acting roles. I got an office job there to tide us over for a little bit. Then we went back to Chicago. I thought maybe I could get a job on a show, or a job in stock, or something. The best offer I could get was for two weeks stock in Zanesville, Ohio for twenty-five dollars a week. You had to furnish your own wardrobe. That was impossible, so I said, "This is ridiculous. We can go hungry in Chicago as well as Zanesville." So, I started trying to get into radio. They weren't dying to have me on radio, either. What did I do for a few months? I don't know if you remember the NRA, the National Recovery Agency. That's when the government hired a lot of people they didn't need just to give them a little money. I went to work in the office of a steel company for sixty-five dollars a month—that's a month, not a week. I was there for six months when I started begging off to do radio auditions. Finally, the boss said, "You've been gone more than you're here. If you leave this time, don't come back." That was my entry into radio.

JASON: You mentioned the NRA. That was the agency that was responsible for the Federal Theatre. They were the ones who kept people like John Houseman and Orson Welles somewhat employed. Let's get back to radio.

OLAN: I started my first radio show in Chicago. That first show was called *Uncle Quinn's Scallywags*. It was a kid's show. I got five dollars for that. Working opposite me, standing on a soapbox, was a kid by the name of Charles Flynn, who later played *Jack Armstrong*. His mother wrote *Bachelor's Children*, a soap opera that I was on at a later date for eleven years.

JASON: You were on several kids' shows. One that everyone knows was *Orphan Annie*.

OLAN: *Orphan Annie* was my first network show. I played the part of Aah-Ha, the Chinese cook on Daddy Warbucks' yacht, who didn't speak a word of English. It was an important job for me, because it paid fifteen bucks. I wanted to make it sound important, so I'd get the scripts ahead, so I could get an idea of what was going on in the scene. Then I'd write dialogue for myself. I'd go to a Chinese waiter friend in a Chinese restaurant and get him to give me the dialogue I'd written in phonetic Chinese. I'd go home and practice it to the barking of my Pomeranian, then make the thing sound really good on the air. The other kid's show I did later was *Jack Armstrong*. I was the second Coach Harding. It was a miserable experience, getting from one show to another. As you probably know, everything was live then. We had no such thing as tape, or wire recording, or anything of the kind. We did two shows a day of everything. We did one show for the Midwest and East, then a repeat for the West Coast. *Armstrong* was from the Wrigley Building on Michigan Avenue in Chicago at three-thirty and four-thirty. *Orphan Annie* was from a mile away, on the nineteenth floor of the Merchandise Mart, at three-forty-five and four-forty-five. My wife would bring a cab to the back door of the Wrigley Building, and I'd run down the steps as soon as I was off the air and run off to the Merchandise Mart. The starter there, and he did it for others as well, would shoot me up to the nineteenth floor. I'd get in the studio door just as Pierre André was droning out the final words of the lead in. I always made it, but the producer would be standing in the control room, looking and wondering.

JASON: You just brought up an important point about the East and West broadcasts. Is it true that you had a problem one time when you were doing *Bachelor's Children* because your watch stopped and you missed the second program?

OLAN: Yeah, yeah. Actually, we had started a club called The Actor's Club. We did all the work ourselves. I was up there working around one day. Our repeat of *Bachelor* was at two-thirty in the afternoon. We had done the morning broadcast at eight-forty-five. I had had lunch and gone up to the club and was working there. The phone rang. It was the director. He said, "It was sure nice of you to be here for the repeat show." I said, "What do you mean? It's not time." He said, "It's time and gone." My watch had stopped. I had completely missed the show.

JASON: Did someone else do the part of Sam Ryder?

OLAN: I think the announcer stepped in, probably Rush Young.

JASON: That sort of thing happened fairly often from what I've heard.

OLAN: It happened occasionally because of a bridge being up. If you had gone over to the Loop to do some shopping and barely allowed enough time to get back across the river a boat would come along. The bridge would go up, and you'd just have to wait.

JASON: There was a show out of Detroit that everybody knows, *The Lone Ranger*. They had one of the best examples of having people stand in because John Todd, who played Tonto, had a real problem with the ladies. He liked all of them. Occasionally he spent too much time with them and just didn't show up. John was about your age now when he was playing Tonto. It was hard to imagine him leaping on a horse. He was eighty-five when the show left the air.

OLAN: I'm not quite that old.

JASON: Sorry, I knew that. I meant at the time when all that was going on.

OLAN: I'm seventy-eight now so this is my sixty-first year in the business. Not bad for a temporary assignment.

JASON: Not bad at all. You've had a long career. Getting back to *Orphan Annie*, there was something funny that always happened on shows like that. It didn't seem funny then, but it does now. They were always giving away things like the Ovaltine Shake-Up Mug. They'd give the mail-in address. They'd just say, "Send your card to *Orphan Annie*, Chicago, Illinois"—that's all.

OLAN: It worked. I'll jump ahead a little bit, and then I want to go back and talk about *Bachelor's Children* and *First Nighter*. In the thirties and forties, there was a kids' show I worked on, not under contract, but from time to time, a recurring character on *Captain Midnight*. *First Nighter* moved me out here in 1947. In fifty-four, we did a TV version of

Captain Midnight, and I was hired on it again. Dick Webb was Captain Midnight, Sid Melton was Icky, his sidekick, and I was "Tot," which was short for Aristotle Jones who was a scientist and lab technician. It only ran a couple of seasons, but I ran into men in their forties, many of whom remembered the show from when they were kids. They remembered it from radio. Last fall we were honored by the Smithsonian Institute. We found fans working there, too. They had us in, took our pictures and then had a V.I.P. reception for us in the National Air and Space Museum. Dick Webb had kept his Captain Midnight jacket. He had been offered $20,000 by some guy in Texas for it, but he didn't want to part with it. He presented it to the Smithsonian while we were there last October, and it's now a permanent exhibit there.

JASON: The character you played on the radio also had a code name SS-11.

OLAN: Right. I did a lot of shows in Chicago. *Bachelor's Children* was one of my favorites, because it ran for eleven years. It was the story of Dr. Bob, who was played by Hugh Studebaker. The doctor's wife, Ruth Ann, was Marge Hannon. They're both gone now. Then there was Helen, the housekeeper and other characters who drifted in and out. Pat Dunlap and I played Janet and Sam Ryder, close friends of the doctor and his wife. The four of us were the constants in the cast. Pat is still out here. She and her husband Dick live up in Berkeley. Some of us are going to get together to do some old radio shows out here at one of the college stations. I've been trying to get her to come down and work with me. I don't know if she'll do it or not. Anyway, *Bachelor's Children* was written by Bess Flynn, who was Chuck Flynn's mother. It ran from 1935 until 1946. In the meantime, Campana Corporation put me under contract for the *First Nighter* program in 1943. *First Nighter* moved to Hollywood in 1947 and continued until 1953, which was about the end of radio as we knew it.

JASON: With just one co-star for almost the entire run of the series.

OLAN: Barbara Luddy, who is no longer living, unfortunately.

JASON: You followed Don Ameche and then Les Tremayne, but Barbara was with all three of you.

OLAN: Don was on for six years, Les for six years and then me for ten years. I also worked for Campana on *Grand Hotel* in Chicago.

JASON: *Grand Hotel* was about the same format as *First Nighter*.

OLAN: It was exactly the same format, just in a different way.

JASON: I was saving *First Nighter* for later, but as long as you brought it up, let's get to it. The show introduction was fascinating because it opened with the announcer saying "Broadcasting from...a little theatre off Times Square," which would be New York, of course. It never did originate from New York.

OLAN: I didn't even know until years later that there really was a "Little Theatre off Times Square." I was there a few years ago. It's next door to Sardi's Restaurant. That was the fictitious location of the broadcasts and as you said, *First Nighter* was never broadcast from anywhere except Chicago and then Hollywood. They were all original three-act plays.

People would submit them on spec. They would be read at the agency by play readers. Then certain ones would be selected and we would do a live reading with a live cast for the agency people to listen and select them. In Chicago, we always dressed. The men wore tuxedos. The ladies wore evening gowns. We dressed a lot in Chicago. On *Chicago Theatre of the Air*, we wore white tie and tails, if you please. On *First Nighter*, when we got ready to move to Hollywood, I had a brand new tailored tuxedo made. I thought I'd really dress up for them in Hollywood. I got out here and never wore it.

JASON: That's not the West Coast image.

OLAN: That's right, sport shirts, etc.

JASON: The Hollywood cast of characters included some very familiar names. There was Parley Baer (Chester from radio's *Gunsmoke*) and Will Waterman, who made the move from Chicago with you. You had Macdonald Carey and a bunch of others, So many people who were interchangeable.

OLAN: Many people now famous were on *First Nighter*.

JASON: I'll come back to *First Nighter*, but you mentioned *Chicago Theatre of the Air*.

OLAN: That was where we brought the male singing stars from the Metropolitan. Henry Weber was the conductor and his wife Marian did the female lead singing. People from Chicago would do the speaking parts. I did many leads.

JASON: The head man of the whole thing was Colonel Robert R. McCormick.

OLAN: Colonel Robert R. refighting the Civil War.

JASON: When most of us would get up and leave the room.

OLAN: We wanted to, but we couldn't. I was at a cocktail party once in his offices in the Tribune Tower—two stories high and with balconies, oh, my goodness!

JASON: Maybe we should explain who he was for those who aren't familiar with his name. He was the owner of the *Chicago Tribune* whose part on the show was to spew his very narrow views on politics between the acts of the light operas and operettas. Now, how about some side stories from *First Nighter*? That was a big show for you.

OLAN: We were on Mutual for a time, but mostly on CBS. One time we were working in a beautiful theatre studio, which is no longer a studio, in the building next to the Tribune Tower. We were in the middle of a comedy. During the first act a guy in one of the front rows had a heart attack. Between acts they came and carried him out. He died. That put a damper on things.

JASON: I guess the show must go on.

OLAN: Maybe he was a critic.

JASON: Let me ask you about a couple of lesser known shows, but first, one that we all know. You were the announcer for a time on *Amos 'n' Andy*.

OLAN: They had some kind of falling out with Bill Hay. I never did find out what it was, but they held an audition. I think half of Chicago circled around the Palmolive Building where the Lord & Thomas Agency was. It was a very big audition, but I got the job. I had become *Amos 'n' Andy's* announcer. They made a proposition. They were going to move to the coast. I got the big sum of fifty dollars a week, and I worked it for two weeks from the very private studio on the twentieth floor at NBC in Chicago where nobody was allowed to even see in except the two boys and me. In the control room was Basil Loughrane, the agency producer, and the engineer, that's all. In fact, the night manager's office had a window into the very fancy studio with a grand piano and a fireplace. The window was covered up during the broadcast so nobody could see in. I did the show for two weeks. Then they got together again with Bill Hay. That was the end of me. He was made the announcer again, and I'm really glad it happened that way, because I would have ended up announcing out here, and I wouldn't have had near the fun that I've had as an actor. I saw Bill around his ninetieth birthday at a Pacific Pioneer Broadcasters luncheon and went over to say hello. He remembered me all right. I said, "Tell me what it was that happened when you were off the show and they hired me to replace you." He said, "What do you mean? What are you talking about? I didn't think I was ever off the show."

JASON: Here are a couple more for you. This is interesting for me, because I have very little information about either of them, just enough to want to know more. One of them was *Grandstand Thrills*, a sports show. The other was *Science in the News* produced by the University of Chicago.

OLAN: *Grandstand Thrills* was for Koolox shaving cream. It was a half hour sports show. It was originated by Dick Wells who was *Ma Perkins'* announcer for years. We did it on WGN Mutual from the eleventh floor of the Tribune Tower. I was the narrator. It was ala *March of Time*. It was episodic. There is a little story connected with that. At the same time as I was doing the show, I was doing a fifteen minute comedy series written by the guy who wrote *Mother's Millions*. It was *The Couple Next Door*, a famous old comedy sponsored by Holland Furnace Company from Holland, Michigan. *Grandstand Thrills* was on the eleventh floor and *Couple Next Door* was downstairs in the new building. *Couple Next Door* was on during the dress rehearsal upstairs of the other show so any changes that were made, any cuts or additions, I didn't see. I left my script up there so they could mark any changes. One night they forgot to make a cut they should have made. I started with a twenty-second lead and went right into the live show. The episode I had been leading into had been cut. I'll tell you, the place really came apart, with people flying into wastebaskets and under the piano to get the pages back that had been discarded. By the time I finished the twenty-second lead in, they had it back together. The episode went on the air. During later episodes, the director came around to each of our scripts and cut enough to make up for what I had unintentionally put back in. The other show, *Science in the News*, was a once a week, fifteen-minute show that I did by myself. It was simply narration with all the up-to-date science news. It was on WMAQ, NBC in Chicago. I would love to get any old records that might exist from it because I had stuff on there about busting the atom; some of the first things that were done that became the bombs that were undreamed of then. The very first of that stuff, I reported on that show.

JASON: Being connected with the University of Chicago, you would have had access to some information that was on the edge of being very hush, hush.

OLAN: I thought I was going to be able to get hold of some of the old scripts or quickie records, the old acetates they used to make. No luck. Out here, I did some shows. I did *Screen Guild Theatre* with Jane Wyman and, of course, more *First Nighters*. I didn't do a whole lot of radio out here. I fell into pictures. In the first one I did for Warner Brothers I was a radio announcer.

****

When I think of Olan Soulé and the movies, I am almost always reminded of one that he did not appear in. It came out in 1987 and was titled, *Radio Days*. The reason I tie him into that picture is because there was a character in *Radio Days* called The Masked Avenger, who, though I may be alone with this thought, I always thought Olan must have been on Woody Allen's mind when he cast that role. The Masked Avenger was a small man with a big voice who fooled listeners because they could not see him. Olan was 135 pounds throughout most of his radio days, but he possessed a booming set of vocal pipes. That was the magic that made radio what it was.

His television credits were endless. He appeared on nearly every top rated show at one time or another in a variety of formats. He did *The Munsters* and *The Addams Family*. He did *Gunsmoke* and *Bonanza*. He did *Dragnet* and *Simon & Simon*. He even did *Twilight Zone*. You name it, he did it.

He was the voice of many animated characters from *Batman* to *Scooby Doo* to *Sesame Street*.

On February 1, 1994 he succumbed to lung cancer after a long and fruitful career.

Act IV: More Chicago Connections

Before we leave Chicago media it would be a shame if we did not bring up two more native Midwesterners who were giants on the air. One was from Central Illinois and the other from Eastern Iowa. Radio may have been king for a long time, but there were also some notable early television shows with Chicago roots.

It would take many volumes to adequately cover all of the people with Chicago connections, so we have to settle for just five of the more memorable. In Act III, we met three of them, Willard Waterman, Les Tremayne and Olan Soulé. Now it is time for another two, or in truth, three, certainly not the least meaningful of the Chicago broadcasting society.

It should be noted that they also ended their careers in California.

Act IV:
Scene One
Wistful Vista

Anyone at all familiar with early radio knows that I have already given away the identity of the subject of this scene. He was a man who gave opportunities to many performers who later made the most of the chances they were given on his show. He was exceptional, when considering the many folks involved in the business, in that his entire career was based mostly on playing one fast talking, sometimes incoherent character, along with his real life wife who always tried to keep him in line.

The show was noted, not only for its cast, but also for a crew of overactive sound men who created one of the best remembered effects in radio history.

The man in question was Jim Jordan and his character was Fibber McGee. We talked on June 5, 1987, not long before his demise. Despite his obvious health problems he gave of his time generously. I feel honored by that.

****

JASON: Jim, your radio career started way back, but before that you and your wife, Marian, were in a form of vaudeville in the Peoria, Illinois area for several years.

JIM: That's not quite true. I was in vaudeville, but we had a concert company, Marian and I. We were not associated with any vaudeville circuit or anything of the kind. We did concerts. We moved every day from one town to another. We had an advance man who sold us. We did everything from twenty minutes to two hours, depending on what he sold in the town. We played small towns, very much like Chautauqua, only we were independent. We had our own company and we did it for three years.

JASON: You were singing and Molly—oops, sorry. I guess it's a common mistake to refer to Marian as Molly after all the years she played Molly. She played piano for accompaniment.

JIM: She was a brilliant pianist and teacher.

JASON: Your radio career began as the result of a bet. That was in Chicago?

JIM: That's the story that goes around, but it's so nonsensical. In those days it was no trick to get on radio. All you had to do was walk in. They'd take anyone who could do anything that could be heard. It was all experimental and nobody got paid. That was the condition radio was in when we started.

JASON: You did get paid on WIBO for the *O'Henry Twins*, your first show.

JIM: Yes, that came a short time after we started, but in those days radio was still something that was experimental, and anybody could get on if they had anything at all they could do. Between that time and the time when we got the *O'Henry* job was less than a year, only a few months.

JASON: You're talking about the middle twenties, and, of course, commercial radio as we know it signed on as early as 1920, so there wasn't much time in between.

JIM: I never heard of any commercial radio in 1920.

JASON: I should have said scheduled radio. I'm talking about KDKA in Pittsburgh and also this station here in Madison, WHA, went on the air at approximately the same time under different call letters. Obviously there were no commercials at the time.

JIM: That's right. The year I'm talking about was '22 or '23.

JASON: You did several radio shows before *Fibber McGee & Molly*. There were *The Smith Family*, and *Air Scouts*, and then the one that led directly to *Fibber*, called *Smackout*.

JIM: *Smackout* was on the NBC network for four years. It was a daytime show. We did a fifteen-minute show five days a week.

JASON: Was that where you met Don Quinn?

JIM: We met Don before we did *Smackout*. He wrote that show from the beginning.

JASON: He did *Olsen and Johnson* before that.

JIM: Yes, he worked with Olsen and Johnson.

JASON: Some other things I'm not too familiar with—I remember *Kaltenmeyer's Kindergarten*. You and Marian played Mickey Donovan and Gertie Gump on that show, with the doctor of utter nonsense, Dr. Kaltenmeyer.

JIM: Marian played giggling Gertie Gump.

JASON: Let's get into *Fibber McGee*. There's so much we could talk about on that subject. Fibber himself was more or less developed earlier from the character on *Smackout*, the same type of character.

JIM: He was exactly the same character as Luke Grey on Smackout.

JASON: Luke was your name on *Smackout* and that name came from a previous show called *Luke and Mirandy*, a farm show.

JIM: They were about the same, but we just did short bits on the farm program as I recall.

JASON: That's going pretty far back. Then *The Breakfast Club*, with Don McNeill came along. You two played Toots and Chickie on that.

JIM: Everybody on radio worked, at some time, on *The Breakfast Club*.

JASON: Fibber McGee was an interesting guy because he never had a job, yet he had a house. He won the house in a raffle.

JIM: No, he never had any kind of a job period, not that I was aware.

JASON: There were so many characters on radio who never worked. Ozzie Nelson was another one, never had a way of supporting himself or his family, but they lived a nice comfortable suburban life, not wanting for anything. We didn't really think about it in those days. It wasn't meant to go that deep. It was comedy and that was all that mattered.

ACT IV: SCENE ONE: WISTFUL VISTA

JIM: That's right.

JASON: Many people showed up throughout the run of the show. It was about four years after the show started that some of the characters entered the scene. I'm thinking first of Bill Thompson. Bill did people like Horatio K. Boomer and Nick Depopolus. Nick was one of the few people, other than you, who could twist words around and get away with it. Something that I always think about is how you could get so many words out in such a short time, all starting with the same letter or sound.

JIM: It was a trick acquired.

****

I had my meals in the kitchen. Kitchenette McGee, I was known as. Kitchenette McGee. The cute and cuddly connoisseur of classy cooking, carefully counting the calories and carbohydrates contained in concoctions of cow cooked in combinations of carrots, cabbage, cauliflower and corn—considerable corn, constant customer of cosmopolitan cafes and corner cafeterias. My compliments were considered to cap the climax of a capable cooks career when I commended kindly on a clever consume' or a keen cutlet and crowned the king of the cakes and crumpets from coast to coast as I cut and carved and cracked and crunched, but excuse us, we're late for lunch.

****

JASON: One of your early characters was Hal Peary as Throckmorton P. Gildersleeve, your next-door neighbor. There was one show in particular that I thought was exceptionally funny. That was the one where you found a watch and you and Gildy were

	taking it apart in the bathtub to try to fix it.
Jim:	I recall that. It was a funny bit.
Jason:	You spent most of the show in the tub with Gildy.

****

Gildy:	Hello there, McGee. Hello, Mrs. McGee.
Molly:	Hello, Mr. Gildersleeve.
Gildy:	What's this I hear about you finding a valuable watch?
Molly:	Yes, we found it at Fourteenth and Oak Street this morning Mr. Gildersleeve. Been advertising for the owner. Show it to him, Dearie.
Fibber:	See, Gildy?
Gildy:	Yeah, the crystal's broken.
Molly:	McGee just did that. He discovered that the molecules are mollycoddles.
Gildy:	He did, huh? You know, I'll bet that would be very funny if I knew what you're talking about. Look, McGee, you bent one of the hands when you broke the crystal.
Fibber:	I did? Which one?
Molly:	The second hand.
Fibber:	The second hand from the right or the left?
Gildy:	Just the second hand, you dumbell...

Fibber: Oh.

Gildy: ...that little tiny hand. Let me straighten it for you, McGee. I've got a steadier hand than you have.

Fibber: Oh yeah? Your hand shakes like a grass skirt at a stag party. I'll do this myself. Lend me your Boy Scout knife. I always was a whiz at fixing watches.

Molly: McGee is part Swiss, Gildersleeve.

Gildy: He is?

Molly: Yes, when he was a little tiny baby, they used him to bait mouse traps.

Fibber: Aah, cut your kidding. Can't you see I'm doing a delicate job here? If I take out this little screw on the side here—

Gildy: Wait a minute, McGee. This is no place to do a job like that. Take it onto the dining room table, so you can keep track of the parts.

Fibber: That's a good idea.

Molly: Look boys, if you're so afraid of losing part of the works why don't you go sit in the bathtub and take it apart?

Gildy: Oh my goodness, what a silly idea.

Fibber: It's not a silly idea.

Molly: It is too.

Gildy: It is not.

FIBBER: Quit arguing with my wife, Gildersleeve. If she says to go sit in the bathtub, that's where we'll go sit...

(Phone rings)

MOLLY: Uh-oh...excuse me. 79 Wistful Vista, Molly McGee speaking. Yes, well can you describe the watch? Yeah, no, no, no, that's a very...nah, that's not a very good description. I'm sorry. (Hangs up)

GILDY: Didn't they describe it accurately, Mrs. McGee?

MOLLY: No, they never said a thing about the crystal being broken or the second hand bent. Just another faker, I guess.

FIBBER: Well, come on, Gildersleeve. Let's get in the bathtub.

GILDY: All right, McGee. Oh boy, this ought to be fun.

MOLLY: Better takeoff your shoes boys. I don't want that tub all scratched up.

GILDY: Ok.

FIBBER: Ok.

GILDY: After you, McGee.

FIBBER: You first, Gildy. You sit in the front end will ya. It makes me dizzy to ride backwards.

****

JASON: There was always a running battle going on between the two of you including checker games

	that could go on for a couple of weeks.
JIM:	Oh sure. Hal was a fine actor and he had a beautiful voice, as did everybody in radio. The voice is all there was. Pretty near everyone in the early days of radio had been a singer before. They all knew voice projection and voice generally. Hal was one of those. He was a fine singer.
JASON:	As he displayed quite often on his own show, *The Great Gildersleeve*. Getting back to Bill Thompson, since you're talking about voice and being able to project characters in our imaginations, he certainly did a lot of different voices, including Wallace Wimple.

****

FIBBER:	Say, how are you getting along these days with HER, Wimp?
WIMPLE:	You mean Sweetie Face, my big old wife? Ooo, about as usual. We had a little tiff yesterday and believe me, Sweetie Face puts up a tough tiff.
FIBBER:	What was it about, Wimp?
WIMPLE:	Oh, it was nothing, really. She came back from downtown with a new hairdo and asked me how I liked it.
MOLLY:	And?
WIMPLE:	I told her. "Well frankly, Sweetie Face," I said, "It looks like an explosion in the excelsior factory," I said… "or a crew haircut with mutiny on the poop deck. I don't blame them for dying your hair like that, but they waited too long to embalm it."

Then out loud I said, "It looks simply beautiful, dear."

****

JIM: Bill was a fine actor. That was quite an important character he did.

JASON: Gale Gordon was one of your side men. He did Mayor LaTrivia and also Foggy Williams, the weather man who always said, "Good day—probably."

****

MOLLY: Ah say does Miss Tremaine ever make any of her own clothes? She always looks so nice.

LATRIVA: Oh, yes, in fact she used to make all of her own clothes when she was starting out on the stage. A young actress has to save money wherever she can, of course.

FIBBER: You said it. Where did Fifi save her money, LaTriv? In her makeup box, piggy bank, top of her stocking? I knew a juvenile one time—used to paste twenty dollar bills under his toupee. He got so rich playing romantic leads that he wore a size twelve hat.

LATRIVA: Anyway, as I was saying, Fifi had rather hard going in those early days. She really had to economize on everything. On trains, for instance, she usually took an upper berth because it was lower.

FIBBER: What was that, again, LaTriv?

LATRIVA: I said, Fifi often bought an upper because it was lower.

MOLLY: You mean a lower berth was higher?

LATRIVA: Higher than the upper berth, yes.

FIBBER: Now wait a minute, LaTriv. I ain't any Einstein in arithmetic so you'd better break it down for me. Which was lower, the lower or the upper?

LATRIVA: The upper was lower.

MOLLY: If the uppers were lower, why did they use those little ladders to get into the uppers?

LATRIVA: Why, because they're higher than the lowers.

FIBBER: You said the lowers were higher.

LATRIVA: Oh no, not higher, no, I meant they were more.

MOLLY: More what?

FIBBER: More higher he means. How much more higher than the uppers were the lowers, LaTriv?

LATRIVA: Oh, stop it! You deliberately try to confuse the issue. I merely stated that Miss Tremaine—

MOLLY: Now, now, now, now, relax Mr. Mayor. Leave us not shriek at each other. Let's argue this out quietly.

LATRIVA: Very well.

FIBBER: Why, certainly. We've all traveled on trains. We all know that you've got two kinds of berths, uppers and lowers. People who are on their uppers can ride on the lowers, because the lowers are higher than the uppers, right?

LaTriva: Yes.

Molly: So, Miss Tremaine could just as well have lowers, because if the uppers were lower than the lowers, the lowers would be higher than the uppers, and the upper would then be the lower because—

LaTriva: I didn't say Fifi lowered the higher upper—the lower heefer—I mean—When I say hoofers were in the lower heeper—When she climbed into an upper on the lower dipper—She will loafer when the liefer will snap—how—lipper—lupper—dipper—shiper—aah—oh—ike—you—McGee!

****

Jason: Arthur Q. Bryan was Doc Gamble and another person who spun off on his own show at a later date, was Marlin Hurt, who played Beaulah. Ransom Sherman was on there occasionally as Uncle Dennis. Isabel Randolph was Mrs. Uppington, and I believe Cliff Arquette played The Old Timer at one time.

Jim: I guess he did, but Bill Thompson did The Old Timer most of the time.

Jason: Bill is the one we remember best, but Cliff did fill in for a short time.

Jim: I believe he did.

Jason: Each one of the Thompson characters had his own catch phrase that we always knew was coming. In fact, all of the characters on the show did. It was something we would wait for. We knew it was coming, but that was what made it funny when it did. One of the people, who was always under your

	skin, was Marian's interpretation of the little girl from across the street, Teeny.
JIM:	She took that character from her daughter, who was probably four or five. She took that from from her.
JASON:	That must have been Katherine.
JIM:	Katherine, yes.

****

TEENY:	Hi Mr., whatcha doin?—Huh?
FIBBER:	Oh, hello little girl. We're just sitting here waiting for watch wanters. What do you want?
TEENY:	I thought maybe you'd come over to my house and play with my 'lectric trains.
FIBBER:	No thanks, just the same Sis, but I wouldn't want to deprive your father of that pleasure.
TEENY:	He isn't playing with it anymore, not since he blew out the fuse.
FIBBER:	Oh, I see. So, you want me to come over and locate the short circuit.
TEENY:	No, I want you to come over and locate Papa.
FIBBER:	I'm sorry I can't make it Sis. I've got to hang around here. What else did you get for Christmas, besides the trains?
TEENY:	I got a lot of things, a pair of skates, and a suitcase, and a Molly Dolly and—.

FIBBER: Hey, wait a minute, what's a Molly Dolly?

TEENY: The kind that says *Heavenly Days!*

FIBBER: What else did you wangle out of Kringle?

TEENY: I got a new game—"Dad Rat It!"

FIBBER: Ahh, now watch your language, Sis. This is a family program. What game are you talking about?

TEENY: "Dad Rat It," I told you.

FIBBER: Now, wait a minute, Sis. You don't seem to know what I'm driving at.

TEENY: What are you driving?

FIBBER: I'm not driving anything.

TEENY: But, you just said—

FIBBER: No, Sis.

TEENY: But, I heard you 'stinctly say—

FIBBER: But I didn't—Look little girl, how about going back to the beginning?

TEENY: All right, ready? Hi, Mr. McGee.

FIBBER: No, no! All I want to find out is the name of the game, dad rat it!

TEENY: That's it.

FIBBER: What's it?

TEENY: I've been trying to tell you all along, the name of the game is "Dad Rat It."

FIBBER: Oh, come now, Sis. There's no such game as that.

TEENY: There is too, I betcha.

FIBBER: Oh, no there's not, I betcha.

TEENY: Oh, yes there is, I betcha.

FIBBER: How do you play it?

TEENY: Everybody gets a card with a lot of numbers on it. Then a man starts calling out those numbers and everybody puts bees on his numbers. Pretty soon somebody says, "Bingo!" Then everybody else yells, "Dad Rat It!"

****

JASON: Marian also played Mrs. Wearybottom, a character that came from an older show, and Old Lady Wheeldeck.

JIM: Marian did all those characters on other shows. We were radio veterans when we started *Fibber McGee & Molly*. We'd been on the air for over ten years. We started *Fibber McGee & Molly* in 1935. We went on radio in 1923.

JASON: Some of those shows were on WENR in Chicago, which is interesting because WENR, for years, shared a frequency on the dial with WLS. Now the only one left is WLS. They had different formats at different times.

JIM: We were on the same wave length as WLS.

JASON: Exactly, they alternated at noon and at midnight. Tell us about the Hall Closet. How did that come about?

JIM: The idea for the Hall Closet started on *The Smith Family*. We had a couch that had a certain spring in it that made a god-awful racket when you sat on it. It always got a big laugh—what we call a running gag. Then years later when we had our own show we were always looking for the same type of thing, something that could become a running gag that people would enjoy over and over. We tried a lot of things, but nothing worked. All of the sudden, one night, Don Quinn wrote the Hall Closet into the script. They'd open the door and everything would fall out. That was the beginning. We thought it went well, so we did it again. We realized we had what we'd had on *The Smith Family*. It was what we had been looking for. Frank Pittman started as our sound man. He was there when it started, but it just evolved from an old show.

JASON: It was a thing that grew and grew as time went on, but it always ended with the tinkle of a small bell and you saying, "I've got to clean that out one of these days."

JIM: It got bigger every time we did it.

JASON: There was a period around 1937 when Marian was in the hospital. You did the show without her and called it *Fibber McGee & Company*. You had someone with you on those, who I always enjoyed, ZaSu Pitts. I think that was the only time you ever worked with her.

JIM: I think you're right.

****

ZaSu: Hello mister, do you need a good cashier?

Fibber: Yes, it's ZaSu Pitts again folks, the gal with a permanent wave in each hand. What makes you think I might need a cashier, Sis?

ZaSu: Well, I thought if you had somebody sitting at the desk—there by the window, you know, somebody with—well, I don't know if I should say it myself, but, you know, a certain appeal.

Fibber: That's a thought, Sis. You need a job?

ZaSu: Oh, not financially, but I thought, now, there's a place for a girl to work and meet some nice men in a refined way. I think sitting there all day long handling money and watching men eat would satisfy both my playgirl complex and my maternal instincts.

Fibber: I don't know, Sis. What experience do you have?

ZaSu: Well, my last experience, mister, was at the public library. A very nice man came up and said, "What're you doing tonight, babe?" And I thought a minute and said, "Well, I'm going home to rinse out a few things. Then I'm going to church for an hour or so." When I looked up, and he was gone. Another experience I had—

Fibber: I didn't mean your romantic experiences. What experience do you have as a cashier?

ZaSu: Well, I've kept my own budget for years and years, mister. I'd show it to you, but it's the same book as my diary, and maybe I might have been a little too frank in a girlish sort of way.

FIBBER: Listen Sis, are you accurate? Can you make change?

ZaSu: I'm sure I can. My grandfather was a lightning calculator and only made one mistake in his life. He calculated lightning wouldn't strike him if he stood under a tree at the golf course. We never found anything, but his niblick.

****

JIM: We came to Hollywood to make a picture. We came to Paramount in 1937. After we got back to Chicago, Marian's illness was coming on. She had it in '37 and '38. In 1939, she came back to the show. I think she was off for about eighteen months.

JASON: *Fibber McGee & Molly* moved to the West Coast about when, 1939?

JIM: Yes, we came here in 1939.

JASON: So, it was one of the first shows to make the move from Chicago to California. So many moved around the middle forties.

JIM: Yes, we came in '39, the later part of January. Marian was not on the show then. She was able to get back on in March.

JASON: There was someone else on *Fibber* whom we haven't mentioned, but he was an integral part of it. He was Harlow "Waxy" Wilcox, who could sneak in a commercial better and faster than anyone else.

JIM:	He was primarily a radio announcer. He did all kinds of commercials. He was a big name.
JASON:	He worked on many other shows, but he became an actual character on yours.
JIM:	We made him a character and did the commercials with him. He had a great knack for comedy commercials.
JASON:	The whole show is a piece of true radio history, Jim. Thanks for talking with me. I'm sure it brought back many memories for many people.
JIM:	Well, it brought them back for me, I know that.

****

When conducting an interview it is normally proper procedure for the interviewer to be brief while allowing the interviewee to do most of the talking. The reason for doing it that way is to learn more about the guest, not the host. In this case I had to make an exception. Due to his failing health, Jim Jordan was not his usual ebullient self so he needed a bit more cueing than is normally necessary. I should have let him off the hook, but he really wanted to do my show. It was almost as if he might have considered it his last opportunity to be on the medium he so dearly loved. For this chance, I am grateful.

It was only a few short months later that he passed away rejoining his wife Marian who left our world much too soon in 1961.

So much was left unsaid. Jim and Marian did several motion pictures at RKO Radio Pictures. In 1941 they did *Look Who's Laughing*. In '42, *Here We Go Again* and in '44, *Heavenly Days*.

When television came along they backed off. The show was attempted with other actors, but it did not translate well to the small screen. It did not make it through the first season.

No one could be Fibber and Molly except Jim and Marian Jordan...

Act IV:
Scene Two
K, F, & O

We often talk about people who could ad-lib when the opportunity presented itself or when they got into a difficult situation because a script had gone temporarily missing or at least a page or two. It was a tricky thing to do considering the time restraints on any radio or television broadcast. Everything was timed to the second in order to get on and off the air on schedule, but, miracle of miracles, there was a lady who worked nearly all of her long career *sans* the benefit of a single printed word.

While she is better known for her work on the tube, she also performed for many years before that on radio.

She was Fran Allison. On May 25, 1987 we had a long chat for *Life in the Past Lane*.

****

JASON: Known first as a singer, then as a country lady with some very strange neighbors and ultimately, on television, where she starred with some unusual characters, who weren't quite like us. This describes Fran Allison. Fran, your radio career began in Iowa. Is that where your singing began as well?

FRAN: Yes, I worked at a station in Waterloo, Iowa, which is just a few miles from La Porte City—WMT. Then, I went from there to Chicago, but while I was at WMT, I developed the character, Aunt Fannie. I thought, when I left Waterloo, she was a thing of the past. When I got to Chicago, my first casting was with Don McNeill on *The Breakfast Club*. That was such a family show that they wanted to know all about you, what you ate, what you wore, what you did, what you saw. Somebody looked into my past and found Aunt Fannie. One morning when we were doing the show, Don said to me, "Fran, what about Aunt Fannie? Is she here today?" I said, "I don't know, I'll see." I turned around and then turned back to him and went into the Aunt Fanny thing. I'm so grateful for it, because she outlasted me as a singer.

JASON: Aunt Fanny was a regular character on the show for many years. She even had her own intro song, "She's Only a Bird in a Gilded Cage." Aunt Fanny had some interesting neighbors. Some of them were Ott Ort, the Smelsers, and Bert and Bertie Beerbower. *The Breakfast Club* was probably the longest running program of its time. It ran for thirty-five years, all the way from '33 to '68, which makes it an even longer running show than *Arthur Godfrey Time*. That one made it to twenty-seven years.

FRAN: It was a part of Americana because it was truly a family show. Don McNeill is one of the most wonderful men who ever lived. He had such an appeal, not only to people his own age. There was such a connection with the audience. We had little groups of Boy Scouts, or Cub Scouts, or Brownies, or Girl Scouts. Then, there would be clubs who would charter a bus trip to *The Breakfast Club*. There were people from industry who listened to the show, many listening in their cars on the way to their particular thing they were involved in. It was difficult to explain, but it was such a lovely thing. I wish today, there could be another such show.

JASON: I remember the audience participation on that show. I remember marching around the breakfast table at home or in the studio, where I attended several of those broadcasts.

FRAN: I know. I used to think, "What kind of a show would I go to where I'd just get up and march around a table?" It wasn't even there, you know.

JASON: But, we really did it. We marched around the table at home and also up and down the aisles in the studio, usually led by Sam Cowling. He was a story in himself.

FRAN: Sam is no longer with us, but Don is well and looking wonderful. I'm going back to Chicago in June on the occasion of the opening of the Museum of Radio and Television. I'll be working with Don again there. It's always such a joy to see him. He's such a good friend.

JASON: Many people got an early career boost on *The Breakfast Club*. I'm thinking now of a couple who were called Toots and Chickie on the very early shows.

FRAN: *Fibber McGee & Molly*—Jim and Marian Jordan.

JASON: Exactly, Jim is still with us out there in L.A.

FRAN: He's a good friend of mine. I see him quite often.

JASON: Another person from the McGee group, who was on *The Breakfast Club* for a long while, was Bill Thompson. He started the character of Wallace Wimple there, although he didn't have that name until 1941 on the *McGee* show. There were some other people who just passed through. Johnny

Desmond was the singer for a time.

FRAN: Who I mourn to this day. He was such an important part of it. There was also Dick Noel, another fine singer, who is still very active.

JASON: And a couple of other singers in a different vein, Homer & Jethro. Also, don't forget Alice Lon, who later became Lawrence Welk's Champagne Lady.

FRAN: And Captain Stubby.

JASON: Gale Page. Patti Page.

FRAN: Yes, Don tells, very often, that when there was a vacancy for a girl singer, Patti Page was on for a week. Don didn't think she quite fit the part. He said, "You can see how valuable my opinions are."

JASON: I've heard some quotes from Cecil B. DeMille about a few actors and actresses that he didn't think would make it, but who did very well in the final analysis. Nobody's perfect when it comes to judging talent. I think one of the most interesting aspects of *Breakfast Club* is that after the first couple of weeks there never was a script.

FRAN: They had to have dramatized commercials. That really grew to be an important part of the medium, but the rest of the thing was all ad-lib. Don was so grateful for audiences because when they would come in, in the morning, they would be given cards to fill in anything they thought was interesting. Out of that came some wonderful interviews. Don was so adept in that department.

JASON: How long were you actually on that show? When did you leave it?

FRAN: I started in 1937. I was on the show for a little over two years. Then I left and went to another network, but I came back in the early forties and continued on until it left the air.

JASON: All the way up to '68. That's a long run for any kind of program.

FRAN: I think it went longer than that, didn't it, Jason?

JASON: I think December 27, 1968 was the last show.

FRAN: I don't think so. I think it went past that time. I know it did, because I left Chicago and went to New York, and I used to commute. I'd go out and work *Breakfast Club* for two weeks and then go back home for two weeks. It was later than that.

JASON: You would certainly know better than I. In 1954, *Breakfast Club* had a brief stint of simulcasts with television. That didn't work out too well.

FRAN: No it didn't, but that was not because of the quality of the show. At the time, ABC did not have as many stations as did the other two networks. In so many instances stations would carry us and then go black for maybe a couple of hours. When the show did go off the air the mail trucks came in heavily laden with protests and letters, but of course, that didn't matter. It was simply an economic issue.

JASON: You had some great announcers through the years. There were many, but at the moment I'm thinking of just three, Charles Irving, Durward Kirby and Ken Nordine, who is still very active on Chicago radio.

FRAN: I saw Ken not long ago. I went back for the instigating of the new museum, and I saw him there.

JASON: Ken does inserts for Public Radio that are on a couple of times a week.

FRAN: He has one of the greatest voices ever.

JASON: And a very strange sense of humor.

FRAN: Yes he does.

JASON: Let's move on to a couple of other radio shows. You worked a little with Ransom Sherman. He's a guy that all the insiders always refer to as a great comedian, but most people on the outside don't even know who he was.

FRAN: He was wonderful. When I first came to Chicago I alternated with the girl singers, one week on *Breakfast Club* and one week on *Club Matinee* with Ransom. We became great friends, as did Don McNeill and I. Ransom retired and was living in Las Vegas. I saw him just a couple of weeks before he died. Throughout the years, our friendship just bloomed and blossomed. I treasure the fact that I worked with him.

JASON: He was always considered a comedian's comedian and a real technician in his field.

FRAN: I think he was a little ahead of the time.

JASON: Were you ever on any of his summer replacement shows?

FRAN: I did two or three of them on radio. Then Ransom went back to Chicago after television came into the picture, and he did a summer replacement there for thirteen weeks or so. Then he left and came back to the coast. Gosh, he was funny. I

JASON: thought he was wonderful.

JASON: I have some *Crest Fallen Manor* shows. That was one of his many summer shots. He also did *Grapevine Rancho* and *Smile Parade*. One of the people who was spawned on *Club Matinee* was Garry Moore.

FRAN: I did Garry Moore's first show on *Club Matinee* when he was the emcee.

JASON: Tell me a little about *Sunday Dinner at Aunt Fanny's*.

FRAN: That was a means of using the various musical groups at NBC at the time. They needed a vehicle for it. I wrote the thing. It was fun to do. It was on at that time on the full Red Network. We had the Red Network and the Blue Network at NBC then.

JASON: And Blue is now ABC, of course. Let's go back even further to one of the earliest soaps on radio, *Clara, Lu and Em*.

FRAN: I did that when they had a later revival of it, wonderful radio show. I auditioned for the part of Clara, but I could have done any one of the three characters because I just loved it. When I was teaching school, I used to listen to it on radio, and I thought it was one of the funniest things I ever heard. The strange part about it was, when they wanted to do publicity pictures of the three of us, Clara was supposed to be a very big, buxom woman. I was, at the time, just about like an ironing board. They had to pad me for the pictures and here were these skinny arms sticking out of this fat lady's apron. It was ridiculous, but I loved it. It was great fun.

JASON: That was a later cast around '45. The show actually started in 1930 with the original cast.

FRAN: The scripts were written by three enterprising girls who were at Northwestern University at the time. When they came back and wanted to revive the thing it was like a cattle call audition for it. I was so glad that I got the part.

JASON: One more radio show, and then we'll move on to the obvious Fran Allison credit. Tell me about *The Peabodys*.

FRAN: That was a short-lived piece with a very fine writer/producer, Les Weinrott. I enjoyed doing it because it was a challenge. You wanted to do everything that came along just to see if you could do it.

JASON: Was that in serial form? It was a fifteen-minute show.

FRAN: They were almost entirely complete episodes. We recorded them at CBS. Where they were played, I have no idea.

JASON: Okay, now we have to talk about the big one on TV that ran for many years and then many more years with specials. Of course that would be *Kukla, Fran and Ollie*.

FRAN: Jason, that really was one of the most beautiful experiences in my life, as far as my work and career are concerned, because it allowed me to live a life of fantasy that I never would have done, had I not been connected with it—and Burr, I truly do love. I admire and respect him. It was an experience too few people are allowed to have.

JASON: The show was mostly just Burr Tillstrom and you, because the other characters were puppets.

FRAN: They never were to me. I knew a little about Burr before we began working together. I so admired his true artistry. Then when we began to work together, there was never a moment when I felt the little people I was talking to were not real. I think that carried over into the show because it never seemed strange to carry on a conversation with a rabbit or a dragon or any of them. It was something for which I'm grateful.

JASON: Is it true that you made it a point to never see the characters, except when they were performing?

FRAN: No, I never would and the little people, whom I loved so much, are in the Historical Society Museum in Chicago. There's a whole wing dedicated to them. I will never go there because I couldn't—I just couldn't, and I'm not being silly about it. I could not bear to see them and know that they could not talk to me or I to them. They were real to me.

JASON: So you never really saw them except when they were animated?

FRAN: That's all. That's how I choose to remember them. Each of them had his or her own personality and I just knew what they'd be like—what they were thinking. Burr and I got to the point where we thought alike. We had no script. We'd have an idea and then we'd just start it out and develop it as we went along. At the time he would say to himself, "I wish Fran would ask this or that," and I'd do it. I would think to myself, for which ever little character I was working with, "I wish he or she would ask me this or that," and they would do it. We just had a wonderful exchange of ideas within each of our heads. It worked out very well.

JASON: The kind of rapport that comes from working together for so long.

FRAN: I guess so.

JASON: That is the next point I was coming to, the fact that the show was never scripted. You're the only person I know of who worked on two major shows, each for long periods of time with no script on either of them. It was all ad-lib.

FRAN: Wouldn't it have been terrible if I had to learn lines?

JASON: And on top of that, both shows were live.

FRAN: Everything we ever did was always live.

JASON: Tell me a little about the little people themselves. Kukla was a sort of everyman character like in the old morality plays.

FRAN: He was the impresario of the theme, and he was kind and he was wise. He could be funny and often times, was a dear thing. I think maybe he and I had a greater rapport than with any of the other characters. Ollie was the sort of person I think Burr would have liked to have been. All of the accolades and praises Ollie received, he just accepted because he thought they were due him. He'd get wild, harebrained schemes, but we just put up with them. I adored Beulah Witch because she was the most enterprising woman I ever met. She came to us from a traveling company of *Hansel and Gretel,* but she left that because she thought she was being typed and she saw the rich promise in the world of electronics. So she decided to come with us. She's a graduate of Witch Normal in North Carolina. We became great friends. She let me be one of the girls on Halloween when her sorority sisters came up from Normal. I got to fly with them. It was just wonderful. How many times do you get chances like that?

JASON: And how many witches do you know who have a broom for dry weather and a mop for when it rains?

FRAN: Of course, of course. And Colonel Crackie was such a gentleman. You got tired of listening to him at times, but then, you forgave him. I just adored Fletcher Rabbit, he was wonderful. Everything changed when you talked with him. We had long conversations. He always made very good sense. He came from Washington, D.C. His mother went into politics, so he had kind of a lonely childhood because she'd be off on speaking trips. She was trying to gain women's suffrage. We told her that her case had long since been won, but that really didn't make any difference. Fletcher was a great gardener and he'd talk to young rabbits. He'd tell them not to go into people's gardens and not to destroy foliage as some of them would want to do, but I don't think he ever really got his case across, because they continued to do a certain amount of damage. We loved him anyway.

JASON: Kukla came very close to not being one of Burr's first characters, because when he made him back in 1936, he was meant to be a gift for a friend.

FRAN: That is right.

JASON: Burr actually had him in a packing case, but after one last look, he knew he couldn't give Kukla away.

FRAN: What actually happened was, Burr was a great fan of any kind of good music and particularly of the ballet. He went to a performance and then went backstage to see a beautiful ballerina. He had Kukla in his overcoat pocket. He put his coat over his shoulders. She was at her makeup table. She looked in her mirror and saw the little guy peeking out. She exclaimed, "Aah, Kukla!" That's the Slavic word for dawn. So that became his name. Burr couldn't part with him after that.

JASON: There's an interesting story that goes with Ollie, too. He was always silent until he performed at the New York World's Fair in *Saint George and the Dragon*.

FRAN: That's also right. Burr used to do a lot of things for junior league groups. He helped them with a lot of puppetry. They wanted a dragon, but not a fearsome sort, one that children would like, so he developed Ollie. What a great thing that was.

JASON: Another character that was developed for a purpose other than the Kuklapolitans was Mercedes, for Marshall Field's department store.

FRAN: She didn't appear there because the theatre that Burr did there was for children. He did that for ten years, but that was a marionette theatre. He continued to do it for one year after we began *Kukla, Fran and Ollie*, but it was just too much, so he gave up the theatre at Marshall Field's. Mercedes lived next door. Then her parents went away for a while so we took care of her at the theatre. You must remember Madame Ooglepuss. I loved her.

JASON: And Deloras Dragon and Clara Kukoo.

FRAN: Clara didn't last very long, and I was glad to see her go, but Deloras was Ollie's little cousin. Her parents were off on a sabbatical leave so she came to stay with us. I came to love her, too.

JASON: The show was awarded many honors before it was all over. Then Burr got another Peabody for the Berlin Wall bit he did on *That Was the Week That Was*, a show that Henry Morgan talked of in depth on my program.

FRAN: It was beautiful. I never see it when I don't cry.

JASON: KFO had later runs on television in different places at different times. It was on PBS and NET and was in syndication as recently as 1975.

FRAN: We did nine years on the *PBS Children's Film Festival*. The last two years I did the narration, but the other seven years we were on camera for it.

JASON: In any event, it was still in production as recently as just a few years ago.

****

On June 13th, in the year of 1987, the Chicago Museum of Broadcast Communications on Wabash Avenue, the first of several subsequent locations, officially opened its doors to the public. On the previous evening there was an invitation only preview. Fran Allison and Don McNeill were both in house. Jim Jordan had also been invited, but was unable to attend. He spent that time at Fran's home in Van Nuys, proving once again that they were, indeed, close friends.

A big surprise, at least to me, was that I also received an invitation at my home in Madison, Wisconsin where I had been working with Wisconsin Public Radio as a private contractor. That gave me a precious chance to spend some quality time with Fran and Don, something I thoroughly enjoyed. On Saturday the 13th, Roy Leonard was doing a remote show on site for WGN, the cradle of many radio masterworks. I was asked to go on the air with him to discuss my Madison based shows *Life in the Past Lane* and *Antique Audio Digest*.

Now, for just a few more bits about Fran Allison. She was an indirect recipient of two Emmys and a Peabody for her work with Burr Tillstrom and their little friends. She has a star on the Hollywood Walk of Fame. She was inducted into the Chicago Television Academy's Silver Circle in 2002, and, along with Kukla and Ollie, was featured on a U.S. postage stamp in 2009.

Fran passed away in 1989. I could say much more, but I think the most cogent thing to note is that she was a very gracious and all around nice person who we would all be grateful to count among our friends.

Incidentally, when she was in Chicago for the museum opening, she remained true to her words. She did not go to visit with her small associates from KFO who are prominently on display there.

Photo Gallery

A Little Early History of the BBC

Cover of *The Radio Times*—**September 8, 1933**
(Stephen Spurrier)

A Little Early History of the BBC

Broadcasting House in the 1930s
(BBC)

A Little Early History of the BBC

Listening in occupied Europe–1941
(Punch magazine)

The British Are Coming

Max Geldray in character
(Max Geldray collection)

The British Are Coming

Max atop his livlihood
(London Times)

The British Are Coming

The original Goons: Harry Seacombe, Michael Bentine, Spike Milligan & Peter Sellers
(BBC)

THE BRITISH ARE COMING

Three men in a tub: Harry Seacombe, Peter Sellers & Spike Milligan
(Sphere Books)

The British Have Come

Alan Young with his favorite pal
(Alan Young collection)

The British Have Come

The young Mr. Young–cira 1946
(NBC)

The British Have Come

And much later
(Bing images)

Throckmorton the Second

Willard Waterman with Shirley Mitchell (Gildy & Leila)
(NBC)

Throckmorton the Second

Mary Lee Robb, Will & Walter Tetley (Marjorie, Gildy & LeRoy)
(NBC)

Radio Idol

Les Tremayne in 1986
(Les Tremayne collection)

RADIO IDOL

First photo with Barbara Luddy for *First Nighter* publicity (CBS)

From Tents to Hollywood

Olan Soulé's first employer (Jack & Maudy Brooks Tent Show)
(Bing images)

From Tents to Hollywood

Part of the *First Nighter* cast (Bob Jellison, Olan, Barbara Luddy & Rye Billsbury)
(Mutual)

Wistful Vista

Jim & Marian Jordan as Fibber & Molly
(NBC)

Wistful Vista

Jim and Marian in a relaxed mood
(NBC)

K, F & O

The Breakfast Club – **Don McNeill with Fran Allison as Aunt Fanny** (ABC)

K, F & O

Kukla, Ollie & Fran
(Bing images)

YOU SAID WHAT?

Henry Morgan and friends on set of *So This Is New York* (1948)
(United Artists)

You Said What?

Henry with Eleanor Roosevelt (his second favorite woman after his wife)
(United Artists)

You Said What?

Henry pokes fun of sponsor
(Bing images)

Gerard

Arnold Stang
(Arnold Stang collection)

Gerard

Arnold and his alter-ego, *Top Cat*
(Hanna-Barbera)

Satiric Jesters

Bob Elliot, Audrey Meadows & Ray Goulding (1953)
(NBC)

SATIRIC JESTERS

Bob & Ray at WNBC, New York
(NBC)

NOT JUST A COWBOY

John Dehner in all his western glory
(Bing images)

NOT JUST A COWBOY

John as Colonel Backscheider on "Tiger Hunt in Paris" (*Hogan's Heroes*) (CBS)

From the Circus to the Plains

Parley Baer – the voice of Ernie Keebler
(Leo Burnett Agency)

FROM THE CIRCUS TO THE PLAINS

Parley in *Air Cadet* (1951)
(Universal)

From the Circus to the Plains

Parley as Chester Proudfoot in *Gunsmoke* with William Conrad (CBS)

Keeping Us Informed

Murrow in *See it Now* studio
(Broadcasting Magazine)

Keeping Us Informed

Lt. Boyston, Murrow and Col. Kelly preparing to head out and report on bombing run
(Janet Murrow collection)

Keeping Us Informed

Ed with Harry Truman in Key West, Florida *(See It Now)*
(Janet Murrow collection)

Keeping Us Informed

Murrow, Fred Friendly and Carl Sandburg
(Janet Murrow collection)

Keeping Us Informed

On the scene making "Harvest of Shame"
(CBS)

Network Impresario

Bill Paley intoducing Jack Benny after he came to CBS from NBC
(Broadcast Magazine)

NETWORK IMPRESARIO

Paley greeting John Kennedy before the Kennedy-Nixon debate in Chicago (CBS 9/26/1960)
(Broadcast Magazine)

Network Impresario

William S before the State Senate Insterstate Commerce Committee (1941)
(Broadcast Magazine)

ACT V:
NEW YORK, NEW YORK

New York City is a place that you can either love or hate. There seems to be no middle ground. It is not for everyone, but for those true lovers of the Big Apple, there is no other place to be. It is a huge megalopolis composed of many nearly autonomous neighborhoods, each with its own distinct characteristics, almost like small towns. The pace is hectic, almost at warp speed compared to most, but not all, other cities in our vast country. However; as the old song says, *If you can make it there, you'd make it anywhere...* Through the years, I had spent a considerable amount of time in New York City and enjoyed it while I was there, but I was always happy to return to my roots in Chicago.

This is the tale of several people who did make it there in a big way in the world of entertainment. Although they were not all native born, they did gravitate to Gotham and spent the bulk of their careers living and working there.

In this act we will deal exclusively with the genre' of comedy, a very specific and testing field, tried by many, but succeeded in by just a few.

I offer here—four of the best of the best.

Act V: Scene One
You Said What?

A quick wit, a master of the ad-lib, a man who could turn everyday events into hilarious situations. He did his best work when left alone to do his own thing his own way. Sometimes it got him in trouble. He stepped on many toes, but in the end he usually produced his intended results. He could make us laugh until we cried. He could also make us think. There was a hidden message behind much of his cajoling.

Who am I describing here? Who was this artisan of the innuendo? He was none other than Henry Morgan.

He allowed me to present his story on *Life in the Past Lane* on October 14, 1986.

Without further fanfare, "Here's Morgan!"

****

JASON: Henry, I know your radio career began in the forties, but could you tell me a little about your background before that.

HENRY: I couldn't have started too much before that. I started as an announcer in the days when everything on radio was live. There were no recordings. I did announcing for a number of years. That led into my getting my own monologue program in New York City some years back. I did fifteen minutes a day, six days a week. It was a combination of what I considered humorful discussions—well, monologues

—I didn't discuss them with anybody—and some peculiar music I found in old record shops. That led into the Second World War. When I came out, I did my own half hour on radio with a cast and orchestra, and so forth.

JASON: The first show was *Meet Mr. Morgan*. Is that correct?

HENRY: It's odd you should know that because we only called it that for about a day, and then it became *Here's Morgan*.

JASON: On Saturday mornings, on WOR?

HENRY: That is correct.

JASON: And didn't you start out as a page?

HENRY: I did start out as a page, but I didn't think that had any bearing on anything. A lot of people started out as pages. I was hired as a page. Well look, now that we're into it, I was hired as a page, and on my way out of the radio station one day I heard some fellows auditioning for an announcer job, so I asked if I could audition. They said, sort of simperingly, "Sure, go ahead." I got the job, but I never knew whether it was because I'd work so cheap or because I'd really won. My salary was $18/week.

JASON: I grew up in that era, and I know that wasn't as bad as it sounds, although it certainly wasn't great, either.

HENRY: That's quite true. You could get by if you lived at home, which I did. I don't know what other people did with their $18. I believe I was the lowest paid. I think the next guy up got twenty. After a while, maybe six, eight months later, I found a better job at another station, and I told them I was leaving. They said, "What are they going to pay you?" I said, "$27," which was true. So I did get raised to twenty-seven. I thought my troubles were over. What would we say these days? That was a quantum leap. That was big stuff.

JASON: Almost a forty per cent rise.

HENRY: I would say so.

JASON: The reason I brought up the page job at WMCA, is because a lot of people think, that by merely being exposed to radio they can land a job on the air, which is very far from the truth.

HENRY: There's more to it than that, if you want to go into it. I was lucky about two things. I had a good voice, but more important, to them at least, was the fact that I spoke good English. That was owing to the fact that my mother was born in San Francisco and I always think that helped a lot. She spoke excellent English, and I learned from her.

JASON: The two most important assets for radio at the time were good grammar and a good voice.

HENRY: It was then.

JASON: Unfortunately, you can get by with almost anything these days.

HENRY: That's true.

JASON: You were on some shows that we well remember, but we don't remember you announcing on them, because it was considered a minor thing, and credits weren't generally given to announcers. I'm thinking of *Lone Journey*, a soap opera, and *Bulldog Drummond*. Dorothy Gordon's *Children's Corner* was another one.

HENRY: How did you know that?

JASON: I have good notes.

HENRY: You have notes I haven't heard of.

JASON: Well, was I right?

HENRY: Yes, but I haven't even heard—! I went into minor shock here because—*Lone Journey*—oh, brother! That was not only long ago, but nobody knows I did it. I didn't know I did it until you brought it up.

JASON: How about a show you worked with Dorothy Kilgallen, Ilka Chase, Sylvia Sidney and Constance Bennett. The name of it was *Leave it to the Girls*.

HENRY: Oh, for goodness sake! Yeah, I worked that a lot. I can't remember the woman's name that ran it.

JASON: Martha Roundtree.

HENRY: Of course. Anyway, what their pattern was—four women against one man, and I loved it.

JASON: You were the defender of the masculine—

HENRY: Point of view on whatever the topic was. That was pretty early, you know, for that sort of thing. I would say it was sort of the forerunner of what later became Women's Lib. It was to show that women are not stupid. That was the basis of it. Of course, they aren't. I look at the whole process as one of long overdue progress. I hate the word progress, because women have been put down for so long. It's not perfect even today, but that's not what we were talking about. I guess it is. I just talked about it.

JASON: Here's another show, one that I don't remember at all, *The Laugh and Swing Club*, where you worked with Morey Amsterdam among others.

HENRY: Listen, Jason, I must admit I'm fascinated. I don't know where you possibly get this material.

JASON: I've been doing this for a long time, so I have many friends in the business. I get a lot of little clues from other people.

HENRY: At any rate, I must congratulate you on your wonderful homework.

JASON: Thank you. It's how I earn my living. Let's move on to *The Henry Morgan Show* and play a little word association game. I'll throw out someone or something and you tell me what comes to mind. First off, Arnold Stang.

HENRY: I still see Arnold occasionally. He played Gerard on the show, and that was one of the reasons for its success, very talented fellow.

JASON: Does he still have that Brooklyn twang he always used on the air?

HENRY: Oh sure, not that bad. He can speak straight if he wants to.

JASON: Here's another name from the show, a young lady who recently died, Florence Halop.

HENRY: Oh yeah, yeah. I don't want to fall into the position of saying they worked for me because they didn't. We worked together. They were the people who made the show possible because I didn't have anything unique about me except my ideas. I didn't sound very comical, so I was lucky when I got the best comics around to work with me. Even Art Carney worked with me for a time. In those days he was known as "Art Carney—who?"

JASON: Art did a lot of radio work. He was with Alan Young at one time, too.

HENRY: And with Gleason when Gleason was doing radio.

JASON: There was something you used to do on all of your shows that was responsible for having you on and off the air from time to time. You didn't do too well with sponsors because you had your own thoughts on them. Let me just mention one and get your comment—Life Savers.

HENRY: That was very simple, and the sponsor was wrong. He was a new sponsor at the time, and I said one night that I took a pack of them home and opened it up. I found the middles were missing, and if he would give me the middles of the Life Savers that he had taken out, I would market them as Morgan's Middles and keep my mouth shut. He was offended by that. I thought that was ridiculous because the audience could remember what I was talking about. That's the whole point of commercials, isn't it?

JASON: It gives much better product identification than just a straight spot.

HENRY: Well, they didn't think so, and that was the end of that.

JASON: Here's another one you had fun with, listen.

****

ANNCR: Now you can be taller than she is.

(Jingle)

Adler, Adler, Adler—Makes you taller—in your elevator shoes. She'll look up to you when you're taller—You can say goodbye to all your blues — Now you can be taller than she is—Here's all you have to do—Just get yourself a lift in Adler, Adler, Adler Elevator Shoes.

****

HENRY: Oh well, that was my, how can I say this?—My lucky client. We had the same problems with that. I wouldn't read straight copy, because I'd been an announcer, and I was tired of reading straight commercials. I thought, if I'm going to be doing humor, how can I do humor one moment and a straight commercial next? It didn't match. I wanted the commercials to match the rest of the show and did them in a light vein. But I had this client, Adler Elevator Shoes, and the plug was; "Now you can be taller than she is." They raised your height about an inch and a quarter or an inch and a half. I thought that was pretty funny because sooner or later the girl would find out. You had to take the shoes off sometime, if this romance was going to work, and she'd know you weren't an inch and a half taller. So, I approached it as I can only refer to as 'my way.' The client didn't like it too much, but his sales picked up immediately. There wasn't much he could do about it except be offended for a while. And the other thing was—I called him

'Old Man Adler.' I didn't know who this man was—never met him. I made up 'Old Man Adler' to give some weight to this...as though there really was someone behind it, when, in fact, there was. He was far from being an old man, and he objected to that too, but it took hold. When people began to say, "You're Old Man Adler," he was sort of pleased. He was selling shoes like crazy, which is, as they say, the name of the game, isn't it?

JASON: It was just sort of a new thing at the time to pick on sponsors. I guess that was the biggest problem with it.

HENRY: The problem was that I invented it, and the first guy usually doesn't do too well.

JASON: Arthur Godfrey did it for years.

HENRY: Well, I happen to know the time sequence there. He had a furrier in Washington, who had a ratty looking fur thing outside the store, and Arthur made fun of that fur being outside the store, which was quite well known. That was about a year after I'd started doing it. He later developed a way of doing commercials that nobody has been able to do since. Arthur's approach was related to mine in that we did commercials as if we were talking to people instead of shouting at them, which was the fashion then. Sincerity is part of it, but that implies that you believe in the product. If you're going to go that way, and I did my whole life, you can't accept products you don't like. Fortunately, I've never had to do that. Even to this day, when I do voice-overs, I will not do medicines of any kind. The only medicine I would do is aspirin, and nobody's ever asked me to.

JASON: You had a lady on your show, not a regular, but she was someone that people would remember for her work with Alan Young and then for a long time with Fred Allen. That would be Minerva Pious.

HENRY: A very talented woman, but not very often on with me. I was lucky I got to use her couple of times, not on any permanent basis. A fine, fine lady.

JASON: Bernie Green did some really wild music on your show, and of course, you were always picking on him.

HENRY: Bernie's music was based on what I picked up from Spike Jones, who was a very inventive guy musically. Spike was a friend of mine. I wanted Bernie, not to imitate Spike, but to get the feeling of what Spike did. He did it with enormous success.

JASON: People don't always realize what a fine musician Spike was.

HENRY: Yes, he was. You have to be very good in order to kid around, you know.

JASON: You can't do anything bad until you learn how to do it good first.

HENRY: That's a principle people should learn.

JASON: You brought up Fred Allen. He had a long career on radio. You were a guest on a memorable show of his, his last show, along with Jack Benny.

HENRY: Quite true. Fred took me on as though he was passing the baton or torch or something. He was my hero and still is. For that kind of comedy he was the best and always will be.

JASON: Here's a short bit from that last show. Fred, more or less, did the intro and then stepped back to listen.

****

FRED: Jack, Henry has to borrow $300 by four o'clock or some skunk at the loan company will take his furniture.

HENRY: Mr. Benny, we thought maybe you could—

JACK: $300—hmmm.

HENRY: I'm a good risk, Mr. Benny. I've been working all winter.

JACK: You worked all winter and you're broke?

HENRY: I'm flatter than something that's been stepped on.

JACK: Mr. Morgan, this is a personal question, but what do you do with your money?

HENRY: Spend it.

JACK: I see your problem. How do you spend your money?

HENRY: Well, after a hard day at work I generally go into a bar. I buy drinks for everybody and then we go to dinner. After buying a few drinks, I suddenly acquire a crowd of friends.

JACK: And you buy everybody dinner?

HENRY: I invited them in. I have to pick up the check, don't I?

JACK: I've heard of it.

HENRY: Well, after dinner the whole gang follows me to a night club. I pay the check and tip everybody wearing a mess jacket. All of the sudden I'm broke. That's why I need $300.

JACK: Mr. Morgan, if you would do as I do you wouldn't need $300.

HENRY: What do you do?

JACK: Well, after a hard day's work I go into a bar.

HENRY: And you buy a drink?

JACK: I faint.

HENRY: You faint?

JACK: A crowd gathers. Somebody gives me three or four brandies to bring me to. I get up off the floor; shake hands all around and move on to dinner.

HENRY: You eat alone, Mr. Benny?

JACK: No, I usually find a group of friends at a table and I sit with them.

HENRY: Who pays for the dinner?

JACK: When it comes time to pay I reach for the check. While I'm slow, sitting around, somebody else picks it up.

****

JASON: I find that the people I talk with from the comedy

field tend to be more serious than people like Arch Oboler from the opposite end of the spectrum.

HENRY: The only thing I know about comedy people, that is good comedy people, is that they have a particular view of life. In order to have it and be able to communicate it, they have to know a little about it. Maybe underneath there's a serious side, only serious to the extent that you really have a feeling about your life and what other people's lives are like. Otherwise comedy is empty. It's just wind.

JASON: It always seemed that, while you were doing your show, nothing was rehearsed. I'm sure that wasn't true.

HENRY: When I was doing the monologues a lot of it was ad-lib, but on the air, no. I mean the half hour show, no. You can't ad-lib when you have a bunch of actors.

JASON: The show always seemed to have a theme as it went along. I remember one on which you were talking about schools on all levels.

HENRY: The theme idea is a good one once in a while. You can't do it regularly because it fences you in. You might have some funny thoughts about, let's say, schools. That's good for ten minutes and then you run out. Sometimes it's productive.

JASON: On that particular show, Arnold Stang was an obnoxious kid in school.

****

TEACHER: Arnold Stang!

ARNOLD: Yeah?

TEACHER: When I address you, I want you to say, Ma'am. Now, will you remember that?

ARNOLD: Yeah—I mean yes, Ma'am.

TEACHER: That's better. Now, for the question. When did Columbus discover America?

ARNOLD: You mean what year?

TEACHER: Yeah—I mean yes. When did Columbus discover this continent?

ARNOLD: Huh?

TEACHER: Not huh!

ARNOLD: Who then, him?

TEACHER: Do not say huh. Say what...What Miss Palsey, what? Remember that. Are you ready for the question?

ARNOLD: What, Miss Palsey, what? Oh, you mean about Columbus?

TEACHER: That's right, about Columbus.

ARNOLD: Aah, Columbus sailed the ocean blue—

TEACHER: Arnold, just look at your hands.

ARNOLD: Huh? I mean what, Miss Palsey, what?

TEACHER: Just look at your hands. They're filthy. Didn't I tell you to wash them yesterday?

Arnold: I did wash them yesterday.

****

Jason: You did quite a bit of television. You did a lot of panel shows, but you also did some comedy. I remember a show that didn't last too long—back in 1970 with William Windom.

Henry: That was based on Thurber stories, James Thurber. It was called *My World and Welcome to It*. The trouble with that show was that it had no control. The writing did not present an opening, middle and a close. It just wandered all over the place. I had mentioned that to the producers. They thought I was just being silly. But people, at least I do…want stories. Even in a half-hour, you have to tell a brief story. On that show, they never did. It just went from anything to anything else and never had an ending. It was too bad, because it had wonderful possibilities. Thurber had written a great deal of material in addition to being a cartoonist. He was a humor writer, one of the best there ever was. If they had stuck with Thurber, they'd have done a lot better. They started to embroider, and they got lost.

Jason: I think your style came a little from Thurber.

Henry: I hope so. By the way, I knew him. We weren't dear friends. I don't think he had any. He got sort of irascible as time went on. His eyesight was failing, which is enough to make anybody miserable, particularly when you're a cartoonist. Toward the end his cartoons were on large sheets of paper. They had to be boiled down. His writing was unique, to the point, so that today nobody can come close to it.

JASON: You worked on all three panels of *I've Got a Secret*.

HENRY: That's where I felt at home. I wasn't just sitting around and having all kinds of things come up that I could work on. It's much better than sitting all by yourself and trying to think of something amusing. When you're on a panel it presents all kinds of ideas. If you think of something funny, that's great.

JASON: Definitely an ad-lib situation.

HENRY: Sure, but you have so many possibilities.

JASON: Here's another television show, one that I remember well even though the run was not that long. It ran here. It also ran in England. It was called *TW3*, an abbreviation for the full title.

HENRY: *That Was the Week That Was.* I loved that show. The show was very daring in its time because it took the news as it was and made fun of it. That went from the President on down. It didn't make any difference who was President. He was always a target. The show was doing very well, even in the ratings, which surprised everyone because it was, let's face it, pretty intelligent. Broadcasters have always mistrusted the audience. Even to this day, some of them still do. They think everyone in the audience is pretty stupid. As I said, *TW3* did well in the ratings and then, for some reason, probably a vice president in charge of sitting around, decided, as they say, to broaden the base. That means to simplify it, make it dumber, okay? So they put on straight entertainment in the middle of a news show that was funny about the news. They put in singers, and I don't know what kind of claptrap, and it immediately fell apart, which is too bad.

JASON: Some things remained the same throughout the run such as having brief intros by the Calendar Girl, Nancy Ames.

HENRY: Yes, I didn't mean Nancy's singing. She was fine. She sang special lyrics every week based on the news, a very difficult thing to do. Not that she made it up as she went along. It was hard enough to write and hard to sing. She did very well at it. One thing interesting about Nancy Ames, for anyone who remembers her, she was born in Panama. If you ever run into her, tell her I said hello and that she was born in Panama.

JASON: TW3 was also aired in England with David Frost as the host. I have to wonder if it was more successful there because British audiences, while we sometimes think of the Brits as stiff, are actually more open to new ideas.

HENRY: The British show actually came first. The American show paid money to the British for the rights to use the same format and title.

JASON: David Frost also appeared on the American version.

HENRY: Yes, he did.

JASON: There were quite a few writers. Burr Tillstrom was one of them. I don't recall that he did any puppet work.

HENRY: He didn't work with puppets. Burr was one of the really creative minds. He did a bit on the Berlin Wall using just his hands. It was fascinating.

JASON: When we think of Burr, the first thing that comes to mind is *Kukla, Fran and Ollie* out of Chicago.

HENRY: Burr did puppet work at the New York World's Fair in 1939.

JASON: If you were to select from your long career, what may have been your favorite thing on any medium, what would that be?

HENRY: It would be something that very few people know about. I did a thirteen-week series locally (meaning New York City) for National Public Television. It was a series of vignettes. They were each about five minutes long. I did about thirty of them—no two related. For example, I did a French chef and I did a taxi driver. I did a lot of stuff and I was free to do them my way. Nobody ever interfered. I loved that best of all, but nobody saw them except maybe twenty people.

JASON: Did you work any of those World War II shows that were done for Armed Forces Radio? I'm thinking of shows like *Command Performance* and *GI Jive* and so on.

HENRY: I worked on Command Performance a number of times. I was stationed in Santa Ana, California, not too far from Hollywood, where they made those things.

JASON: There was so much done on Armed Forces Radio. There was no end to the talent, and everyone worked free.

HENRY: Well, why shouldn't they? You know, it's a funny thing. I have wondered, from time to time, why actors and people like that are expected to work for nothing for benefits, but for the war effort, that was something else again. That *was* for our own benefit.

JASON: One more question, what is Henry Morgan doing these days to keep busy in your own town, New York City?

HENRY: One thing is voice-overs. A lot of people do not know to this day what that means. When you see a commercial on television and you hear a voice talking about stuff, but not on camera, that's a voice-over. I do that kind of work. And then, my wife and I are doing a book called *A Child's History of the World*, which I have written, and she is illustrating. We haven't shown it to a publisher. I must say, it's very good. Somebody will like it.

****

Henry Morgan was a complicated man with a sometimes stand-offish personality which prevented him from having a great many close friends. He had a hard time accepting success and often did things to ruin his own prospects. He could get exasperated at times causing him to sulk.

That is not to say that he was not respected for his humorous, satirical work by many of his broadcast and writing brethren. As he stated, Fred Allen was always his idol. His admiration was reciprocated by Fred. Some others who greatly appreciated Henry's overwhelming ability to entertain were the aforementioned Jack Benny and also Fanny Brice, Robert Benchley, Red Skelton and Dave Garroway.

At one point in his career he was honored by being selected by Norman Corwin to play a major role in one of Norman's satires, "Descent of the Gods." That was in 1941. Anyone familiar with Norman's monumental contributions to radio history would know that that was indeed an honor. Norm's selection of actors was never random.

In the fifties, Henry wrote briefly for *Mad Magazine*, and his byline could also be found in several other national publications.

It is an unquestioned fact that Henry Morgan was a genius in his chosen field of endeavor. Lung cancer took him from us in 1994.

ACT V:
SCENE TWO
GERARD

It seems appropriate to follow Henry Morgan with one of his long time sidekicks on the airwaves. There was much more to this man than just that. He once described himself as *a frightened chipmunk, who spent too much time in the rain.* He always said his twangy Brooklyn delivery was like a trademark for him. That term could also be applied to his oversize horn rim glasses.

He handled comedy lines in his own inimitable fashion, but he also did some very serious dramatic work.

His name was Arnold Stang. On June 20, 1987 he appeared on *Life in the Past Lane.*

****

JASON: Arnold, You started on radio at a very early age.

ARNOLD: That's right. I was about nine years old. I started doing *Let's Pretend* and *The Children's Hour*, programs like that, and I haven't stopped yet.

JASON: Still going strong.

ARNOLD: Yeah—right.

JASON: *The Children's Hour*, you're referring to was *Horn and Hardart?*

ARNOLD: It was *The Horn and Hardart Children's Hour*. It was on, on Sunday mornings. I would do *Let's Pretend* on Saturday mornings. My folks didn't even know I was going to do anything on radio, so when they found out, they weren't too sure. I didn't realize that people don't get to start in this business with a professional job. So, when I said they offered me a job doing *Let's Pretend*, which was the most sought after children's show in the country, they said they weren't too sure they wanted me to do it, but it would be all right if it didn't interfere with school. I could only work on Saturdays and Sundays.

JASON: If you combine the running time of those two shows you come up with about sixty years. A lot of people got their start on one or both of those shows.

ARNOLD: They were great breeding grounds for people who went on to do famous things.

JASON: What was your first teenage role? Would it have been on *The Goldbergs*?

ARNOLD: I started doing *The Goldbergs* after I was doing *Aunt Jenny's Real Life Stories* and most of the other shows while I was still in the latter part of the period when I was doing *Let's Pretend*. I just started doing other things. I was working during the week too, after the initial couple of years. When I got to be about eleven, I started to work in the middle of the week. I did everything, including working with people like Al Jolson and Eddie Cantor or whoever came down the pike. I got to do things with people like Arturo Toscanini, and I did General Motors commercials. I did whatever came along. There were a lot of series. I did *Easy Aces* steadily and *Dr. Christian* for a time, *Death Valley Days, Cavalcade of America.* I used to average four or five shows a day. After a certain period, I started to do plays on Broadway, which led to films. During the time I was doing films, I got my own show replacing Jack Benny for the summer with Edna May Oliver playing my aunt. She was also very active in movies.

JASON: That was *The Remarkable Miss Tuttle*. She was a lady who could solve everybody's problems but her own.

ARNOLD: I'm not sure that was the name. It was a very long time ago.

JASON: The show I'm thinking about also featured Lillian Randolph and Cy Kendall.

ARNOLD: I remember Lillian played a maid on it. Anyway, I did a show similar to that the following year, called *That Brewster Boy*. That was in Chicago. I would have to take a train back to New York to do *The Goldbergs* and *Easy Aces*. Then I'd go back to Chicago, on Thursdays and Fridays, for *That Brewster Boy*. We'd rehearse on Thursday and be on the air on Friday.

JASON: So you were part of the "Bridges Up Club" in Chicago.

ARNOLD: Right. That was the greatest excuse in the world. Whenever you were late it, "…the bridge was up." Well, what you see, in New York, what I used to do—I was trying to do so many different shows that very often the schedule was a little tight and I would be late. I carried a pack of Band-Aids with me and I'd stick one on my forehead and say I was in a cab that hit another car. That was my excuse. I'd blame the traffic.

JASON: In those days radio people were working so many shows, whether it was Chicago or New York or Los Angeles. Schedules were so tight that it wasn't too unusual to miss a show.

ARNOLD: As I said, I used to average four or five shows a day, sometimes as many as eight. I had several people working for me. I would never rehearse. I'd come in, and they'd give me a script all marked up, and I'd go in and read it for the first time on the air. It had been properly cut and marked, so that I could read it straight through. I would just pay those people the rehearsal fees. It was very good for them because very often they were people trying to break-in, so a lot of directors got to hear them work because they were reading my lines while I wasn't there. It was similar to a surgeon who comes in at the last minute after all the preparations are done. He does the final cut and then leaves. Then his staff finishes up. At least that's the way it is in fiction. I don't know if it really happens that way. Orson Welles had a way to solve scheduling problems. He had a private ambulance. He used to go from show to show with the siren blaring, whizzing through traffic. He'd be on 40th Street and Broadway, doing *The Shadow* and then he'd zoom to 53rd and Broadway and do the *Phillip Morris Show*, or he'd be on Madison Avenue at CBS doing something. He always got around real fast. He was also doing theatre.

JASON: He was involved at The Mercury Theatre with John Houseman.

ARNOLD: He was, but when he got more deeply involved with it, he pretty much gave up radio. It was just too much to do—even though many of the actors at the Mercury were doing radio as well. When television came on you couldn't double as much. You could only do one or two shows a week, except for daytime soaps. I was doing a one hour daytime show in those early days called *Captain Video*. We rehearsed and did a one-hour show every day, which now seems okay, but there was a period when they thought it was a most unusual thing to do. They were used to rehearsing a whole week to do a show. We'd read through the script then go home. We'd come back in the morning and read again, then go down and rehearse on the set, and then do it. It was amazing that we could remember all those lines.

JASON: But not always did everyone remember their lines.

ARNOLD: There was one man, a character man, who often had trouble with his lines. His trick was to just keep talking. He might have been in the middle of a highly technical thing about the space ship. Suddenly he would say, "You know, I had the most delicious fruit salad today," and he would go on talking about what he ate for lunch or the suit he was wearing or whatever. People just accepted it. They didn't seem to realize that he had gone far away from the subject. It was all fun.

JASON: I assume that would be called stage presence.

ARNOLD: It was a very good trick, just keep talking.

JASON: In the recent past I've had a couple of guests on this show that you worked very closely with. One was Alan Young. The other was Henry Morgan. Which one of those gentlemen did you meet first?

ARNOLD: It's so hard to say. The whole period sort of blends together. I was working with everybody around the same time. If I was to guess I would probably say I worked with Alan first. Henry was still doing his one man, fifteen-minute show when he decided he wanted to have a variety show with sketches. I started working with him before it went on the air. We did a sort of test run before it was sold. I had a very long relationship with Henry. I think that was one of the best shows ever done in any medium. He was absolutely a genius. He had a tremendous influence on all of broadcasting. People who worked on that show, writers, directors, actors, and so on had immediate entrée to anything. Writers would go from that show to *The Jack Benny Show*, places like that. It was so far above the caliber of radio comedy at the time. It was really a remarkable show. He deserved all the success he had then. The only thing I was sorry to see is that he didn't continue it on TV. We did a couple of years on television and then he went to Europe. When he came back, he went back on radio. I think at one time he was doing one of the panel shows.

JASON: He did *What's My Line* and *I've Got a Secret* for a number of years. He told me they were a good format for him because they were strictly ad-lib. Alan Young told me that when the part of Hubert Updike III came up, a role eventually played by Jim Backus, that you were auditioned for it. Remember that?

ARNOLD: No, I don't, but I'm sure I must have. At that point, I was doing almost anything they asked me to do, and in some cases, I did things that I would never be identified with now. I'm sure there were many different characters on that thing with Alan. On any of those shows, you had to be able to do different characters. When I was working with Henry, I had about four or five different running characters on every show. I was doing the German, the Professor, the Cockney, two Hillbillies and, of course, Gerard, the New York skeptic. Johnny Carson had a variety show. On that, I was doing a Spanish guy, a German, and a kid from Brooklyn, kind of thing. I also did an English snob. On *The Goldbergs* on radio, I did a running character called Seymour, who was on almost every day. In addition, I played the chauffeur and a Russian director. I played a ninety year old Jewish tailor who spoke with a heavy accent. It was not at all unusual to do two or three different characters on a single show. Very often there would be as many as ten characters and there would be only three or four people in the studio. The two leads didn't double at all, so the other people had to play all the other parts. It never fazed me or any of the other people. It was part of the package. You just played whatever you were asked to play.

JASON: I think that was an advantage in being a character actor where you weren't necessarily identified with a particular character or voice. You could do many things and no one would know it.

ARNOLD: On every one of those shows, there was always at least one character that would be highly identified. There would be magazine pieces about them. People would ask me to do that character on another show and things like that. In addition, people very often would like two or three other things that were on that show and never identified me with them. They would identify Gerard on the *Morgan Show* or Francis, who I did on a radio show with Milton Berle. I worked with Berle on radio a long time before he went on television. Originally I was his son. Even on that show I would sometimes double. He would do a man on the street thing, and I would be the man. I'd come in as a Broadway sharpie, or a hillbilly, or whatever. You developed this flexibility, which also helped greatly in the theatre. You'd read a part and decide how you wanted to play it. Very often they'd pick out a characterization that you'd used in a series somewhere, and then you'd develop it for the theatre. Naturally, you'd also have to develop all the body movements and the facial expressions. A lot of it was internal anyway. Radio was a tremendous challenge. You had to do everything with your voice. You had to paint the set. The makeup was all in your voice. You gave people a complete stage in their minds. You had no makeup or costumes. That was also great for developing your concentration. It gave you the ability to develop the instrument that was your voice.

JASON: At the same time it developed the intelligence of the audience because what you were doing was interpreted many different ways by many different listeners.

ARNOLD: Unlike television, radio depended on the intelligence of the audience. Television depends on the thought that the audience knows nothing. They have to explain everything to them. They have to completely reduce everything to a predigested concept of some kind. Fred Allen called it "chewing gum for the eyes." That's true, although I really enjoy doing television, and I enjoy watching it, too. It's just entirely different. It's all done on an entirely different basis. It's like some newspapers believe, that until something appears in that paper, nobody knows about it. So, they must thoroughly report whatever they print. They feel that when they print a report, or an article, or any news item, it has to be fully done because, until it appears in their newspaper, nobody knows about it. The same thing is true for television. Until they tell you, you don't know what it's about. Somebody would say, "Now there's the door," and then read what it says on the door. They work from a different standpoint. They have a different way of presenting their product.

JASON: Even more so than on film. On film things are more normal than they are on television. They're not as forced.

ARNOLD: Film is really an extension of the theatre. It depends on the audience, and in most cases, is trying to reflect life, an extension of life. They are showing you an experience or sharing an experience with you. I think, with television, it's closer to providing you with some sort of visual entertainment, not really sharing the same kind of experience, in most cases. I always think television is a descendant of the old. In the old days, they used to go out with a wagon with a sort of platform on it—sort of a buckboard tongue that came out. Then, they'd have someone come out and play the banjo and sing, or dance, or an Indian do an Indian dance to attract the crowd. Then they would sell you calico, or medicine, or needles and thread, books, or whatever they had. Television does the same thing. They come out and dance, or do a sketch, or play some music. Once they've got your attention they try to sell you something. It's primarily a sales medium. I think television is more related to the old medicine shows than it is to the theatre.

JASON: There's one form of television that's a little like radio in the old days, in fact, a great deal like it. It's something that you have done on many shows. I'm talking about animation. You worked on *Popeye* and you also did the lead on *Top Cat*.

ARNOLD: I still play *Top Cat*. It's still on. I just did a two-hour special of *Top Cat*. I've done a lot of animated shows. While I was working on *Popeye* I was also Herman the Mouse on a Paramount cartoon series, *Herman and Katnip*. Those were done for theatres, but later appeared on television. Very often it would be the same day as *Top Cat*. I would do a cat and a mouse every week. Then, of course, I did *Courage, the Cowardly Dog*. I did some theatrical animated films, too, like *Raggedy Ann*. I did *The Aristocats* for Disney. There must be eight or ten theatrical films I did. I still do voice-overs for animation. I did a lot of Friz Freleng things, *Mister Jaw, Little Lulu*, and I can't remember all of them. There were so many.

JASON: A bunch of classics.

ARNOLD: For Hanna-Barbara I did other things along with *Top Cat*. *Wait Until Your Father Comes Home* was one of them.

JASON: Speaking of films, you've made quite a few movies, but there are some that stand out. One of them would seem like a very different kind of character than you normally played, but you played all kinds. It was Sparrow in *Man with the Golden Arm*.

ARNOLD: Wonderful character. I got a great deal out of it. It was different, and yet it had a lot of things that I had done before. It was sort of a combination or distillate. Originally, when the book was written, I was approached about playing Sparrow from the galleys. They were going to do it as a film with John Garfield. Then John pulled out and it stood in limbo. Before they had the book published they decided I was Sparrow. They were going to do it on Broadway. I was going to do it on Broadway with Marlon Brando, Maureen Stapleton and Peggy Ann Garner, a terrific cast. Kazan was going to direct it. Meanwhile, Otto Preminger bought the rights, offered me the part of Sparrow in the film and in some way prevented the play from being done. I thought the play, which was written by Jack Kirkland, who also wrote *Tobacco Road*, was far superior, although the screenplay was an excellent one, one of the best I've ever read. The stage play had many interesting things that the film didn't have. Anyway, Preminger prevented them from doing the play. I went into another play called *No Time for Sergeants*. I had already signed to do the film. He advanced the schedule because Frank Sinatra had his own schedule problems. He had just finished *From Here to Eternity* and had to do another film after this one. So Preminger pulled me out of the play. I never did *No Time for Sergeants*. He pulled me out of two plays, really, because he quashed the production of *Man with the Golden Arm* as well. This is a long way to say, I really looked forward to doing it, and I thought there were a lot of many characters in it that I had played elsewhere. One of the things it reminds me of is that I had worked with Frank on radio when he first broke away from Tommy Dorsey. He had an unsponsored radio show on CBS. He asked me if I would come on and play his crony. Then later, he started doing other things. On his first television show, he asked for me, so I was on it with him, and Peggy Lee, and Bob Hope. He kept asking me to play this character with him, so when he started to do Man with the Golden Arm, he thought I was the one for Sparrow, not knowing that other people had already said the same thing. He just thought that I was the one. It came as a big surprise to him when he found out that other people had spoken to me about doing it before that. He's always been a good friend of mine, and I've always looked up to him. I've always thought that he was a tremendous talent. He was one of the loyalist people I've ever known. If he is your friend, you'll never have anyone more on your side.

JASON: When he did *Man with the Golden Arm* his career was on a big upswing.

ARNOLD: Right, it was right after *From Here to Eternity*. That was his turnaround. That's when his career turned back upward. He got a tremendous amount of recognition from that. It was straight up from there to when he became "The Legend," even though he had a few legendary exploits before that. He had been like a skyrocket and then he leveled off, so he was on a plateau. Things didn't seem to be progressing much. He stayed on one level, and then he turned it around. It was very smart of him. He had been primarily a singer and a variety performer. He showed he could be a very good actor as well. His singing always proved it. The most effective part of his singing was the fact that he had this tremendous ability to project a mood. That is what we actors spend twenty years studying to achieve. He was a natural actor. He projects a great emotional stream, whatever the mood may be, sometimes very melancholy, sometimes very romantic—almost erotic at times.

JASON: Your career has been very busy. You've been in a lot of film, Broadway, and radio productions, you name it, you've done it. What is on the scene for Arnold Stang today?

ARNOLD: I've been doing some theatre. As a matter of fact, I was supposed to go to Chicago to do *Sugar Babies*, until I realized they wanted me for an extended period, and I couldn't go for that long. I do some summer theatre, and during the winter I do some plays. I do a lot of voice-over work, and I do some commercials. I recently did *Tales from the Darkside* on which I played a three-thousand year old mummy. It starts out very scary and turns very cute later. I do some TV guest shots. I still do *Top Cat*. I did about thirty-three of those last fall. I guess I'll be doing more this fall. Other than that, I mostly free-lance. I have fun.

****

And I had fun talking with Arnold. In many ways he was typical of all of the celebrities I have spoken with, courteous, cooperative and entertaining. He surprised me when he did something no other interviewee ever did. When I finished interviewing him he turned the tables and proceeded to interview me. That made me feel very good. It was so unexpected. I found out that I was more interesting than I ever thought I was, but I will not bore you with that. I only regret that the recorder was not still running at the time.

Mr. Stang did many movies. It is hard to forget a small role he played in *It's a Mad, Mad, Mad, Mad World*. His partner in that one was Marvin Kaplan, a very similar personality. Maybe the strangest partner he ever had on film was Arnold Schwarzenegger in *Hercules in New York*, Schwarzenegger's first screen work.

Two of his more memorable TV commercials found him as the voice for Chunky Candy Bars and the voice of the Bee for Honey Nut Cheerios. There were many more. The man always kept very busy.

Arnold Stang died of pneumonia a few days before Christmas in 2009.

ACT V:
SCENE THREE
SATIRIC JESTERS

Off the wall? Wild and crazy? Unbelievably creative? They were a duo who played off each other to perfection like no other combination that comes to mind. They jabbed at everyone with no exceptions. No one and nothing was a sacred cow. It was all in fun and rarely offended anyone, in fact, in most cases the victims were flattered to be remembered. Old radio shows were one of their favorite targets.

Both were natives of Massachusetts who began their careers in Boston, but soon found their way to New York City radio and for a time, television, where they spent most of their five decades on the air.

They were Bob Elliott and Ray Goulding, usually referred to simply as Bob and Ray. We enjoyed a mostly three-way chat on October 6, 1987.

****

JASON: You both started the way many do, with variable success. Bob, you were a disc jockey and Ray, a news reader. Often those two elements banter back and forth on radio today, but you two guys went way beyond that on WHDH.

BOB: As it turned out, we did. We didn't really have any plans to have it work out that way, but we're happy that it did.

JASON: That was in Boston where you're both from originally. At the same time, you were doing some pre-game shows for the Red Sox. I would imagine it was not standard baseball fare the way you did it.

BOB: We did a lot of sports oriented stuff, along with just poking fun at radio in general.

RAY: We did an early morning program and also a program before the baseball games.

JASON: They would have been at about the same time, right?

BOB: Yes, we did them both. We did the morning show and then we did the pre-game.

RAY: We were both staff announcers too. It was a lot of work.

JASON: That would include many of the same characters you're still doing. I would imagine that Wally Ballou was one of the first.

BOB: Yep, he started things, along with Mary Magoon.

JASON: Charles, the poet?

RAY: Yup!

JASON: Here's Charles.

****

BOB: Around the corner and up your street comes the friendly poet, Charles, to read again from the tattered pages of his manuscript, bring forth a poem of nostalgic memories, something for all of us to listen to and dream by. Here is Charles.

RAY: Hello, this poem is called "Memories." The rain has turned to tears, and I've been terribly, agonizingly lonely these many years. And I've only had two beers. *(breaks up)*

BOB: Charles, Charles, please!

RAY: The night we kissed and said goodbye, when our happiness took wings as if to fly—Make that water with that rye. *(breaks up again)*

BOB: Charles, please, please!

RAY: I took your hand in mine, our love to begin. That guilty feeling, that innocent sin—and just a touch of gin. *(riotous laugh)*

BOB: I'm afraid we can't go on this way, Charles. You want to try it once more?

RAY: Let me try one more from the top.

BOB: From the beginning.

RAY: The rain—*(more laughs)*.

BOB: I'm afraid we have to call a halt to this, Charles. Until the next time he comes around the corner and up your block, Charles, your friendly poet philosopher says—

RAY: So long now. *(can't stop laughing)*

****

JASON: Didn't your network careers begin in New York, around 1951?

Bob: We had a man, who became our manager, who had heard us in 1951. He engineered the move.

Ray: He got us a contract with NBC. That's why we left Boston.

Bob: He sent it to us in Boston and we said sure, we'd like to do it. So we went to New York and did a daily fifteen-minute show, as well as an hour on Saturday on the network. A few months after that, we took on the local early morning show on the NBC station there.

Jason: It was through Bob Berry that you got on NBC?

Bob: Bob Berry was the guy.

Ray: He was in charge of programming, head of programming at NBC.

Jason: Vice president in charge of programming, I believe, what is now called program director. You went from a fifteen-minute format, then a thirty-minute program, another fifteen-minute shot and later you showed up on *Monitor*. A lot of people did *Monitor* through the years.

Bob: We were there the first day *Monitor* went on the air. One of the other New Yorkers was Henry Morgan, and the list goes on.

Jason: How did some of your characters evolve? Was it pretty much ad-lib?

Ray: It was, because we didn't have time to write, along with everything else we had to do as announcers, so we just sort of fell into them.

BOB: We were lucky, I guess. We just saw fun situations around us, things that happened at the studios. That was the basis for much of what we do.

JASON: Much of your material is derived from old radio shows, soap operas, and such.

RAY: Those were written by Joseph Biden. We don't know where he got them from.

JASON: Would you say most of his material came from you?

RAY: We almost did.

JASON: Parts of what you did were taken from real life situations as well as from old radio shows.

BOB: Oh sure, radio was our whole thing.

JASON: I'm thinking about things like *Mary Backstayge, Noble Wife*.

BOB: We also did a lot of sports commentaries, newscasters, and on the street people.

RAY: It was all radio oriented. We planned on doing a lot of different mediums. We did Broadway. We did Carnegie Hall a couple of years ago. We did TV, and we did stock way back, when we first came to New York. Along with all of our radio schedule, we also did a fifteen minute TV show, when we didn't have sets ourselves.

JASON: When you were doing one of your shows in New York you were on opposite Gene Rayburn and Dee Finch. I understand they topped the ratings until your show outdid them.

BOB: It was good competition for all of us. That was a local show we did for NBC. They were on a different station.

JASON: You've done a bunch of commercials through the years. I have a series of them in mind where a moose became a deer or whatever else.

RAY: Hartford Insurance. We're still connected with them. We do spots occasionally.

JASON: I used to dub those commercials for Hartford at a station I once worked for. *It's a moose* became a kind of catch phrase around there, because it was never really a moose.

BOB: There were a lot of those antlered animals we never heard of, as a matter of fact.

JASON: I did an interview with someone a long time ago who was the originator of a show that you did a take-off on which you called *One Fella's Family*. I'm talking about Carlton E. Morse. He mentioned how much he enjoyed what you did with his series, *One Man's Family*.

RAY: Really? I never heard that. We never got any feedback on that. We did it for years.

BOB: Yep, down by the sea wall.

JASON: And up on the mountain, near San Francisco.

RAY: We paraphrased most of the characters. That was a favorite show of ours.

JASON: *Mr. Trace, Keener Than Most Persons, Dr. Ok, The Sentimental Banker, The 64 Cent Question,*

Jack Headstrong, the All American American?

BOB: Those are things that most people don't remember the originals of now.

RAY: So we've gotten away from doing specific takeoffs on our Public Radio series. Most of the dramatic things we've created for that are like *Garish Summit*, which is more or less a parody of TV shows like *Dynasty, Dallas* or *Falcon Crest*.

BOB: If you do a *Mr. Trace* now, nobody knows what you did.

RAY: Of course, that's fifty years old, that program. The original was back in the thirties. We were just kids.

JASON: I've spoken with some of the people who were on the originals. One was *Jack Armstrong*, not *Jack Headstrong*.

BOB: Jim Ameche.

RAY: Jim was the original.

JASON: Jim was on it, but so was his brother Don. It got to a point where they sounded too similar. Jim is gone now, but Don is very much still around.

BOB: We worked with Jim here in New York for a couple of years at WHN.

RAY: In the seventies.

JASON: One of your routines that used to break everybody up, and I'm sure you still do it occasionally, was "The Slow Talkers of America."

Bob: That's what we're doing now.

Ray: I guess we had heard someone talking that way at some time, so he became one of our characters.

Jason: I can think of people I have known who I just wanted to pry the words out of, because they never finished.

Ray: Yeah, you could wait light years before they got to it.

****

Bob: This is a surprise time for me because, I've got an opportunity to meet and talk to my next guest. This says here, *in our times, in dining rooms for years*. I don't know if that has any special meaning to you. Just sit there now and tell me your name.

Ray: Harlowe——P.——Witkin.

Bob: And where are you from?

Ray: From——Glens——Falls——

Bob: New York?

Ray: New——York.

Bob: And what do you do there?

Ray: I——am——the——president——and—— recording——secretary——of——the—— S.——T.——O.——A.

Bob: What does that stand for?

Act V: Scene Three: Satiric Jesters

RAY: The, uh———slow———talkers———of—America. We believe———

BOB: In speaking slowly.

RAY: In———forming———

BOB: Your words and thoughts?

RAY: Our ideas———and—opinions———slowly before———speaking———We are here———

BOB: In New York City!

RAY: In the———city———of———New York——— attending———our convention,———our——— annual———

BOB: Convention!

RAY: Convention.———All of our———members,———all two———hundred———

BOB: Members!!!!

RAY: And fifty———

BOB: Members!!!!

RAY: Members, are———here———speaking———

BOB: Talking slowly! That's understood!!

RAY: Our credo———

BOB: Is to speak slowly!!

RAY: Goes—something———like———this———

****

JASON: In about 1962 you were doing a four-hour show. Was that mostly your regular routines?

RAY: We played some music.

BOB: Our vocal chords couldn't handle four hours.

JASON: Plus news breaks, I'm sure.

BOB: Yeah, it was a morning show. It was something that not too many people had done, in that we'd tape it in the afternoon before and leave holes for weather and news and everything. People thought we were there every morning. One day a week we agreed to come on live just so we could say we weren't always on tape.

JASON: I think what's interesting is that you started out on radio and, at that time, it was still going pretty strong. It wasn't too long after that that, that radio faded away and yet, you're still working on that medium today. Not many people can say that except maybe Steve Allen.

BOB: He came back to radio just this last summer. What you say is true. We always liked it. It was the medium we wanted to get into. Television just followed.

JASON: On radio you could use all those characters and you didn't have to worry about makeup.

RAY: We do make up though, over our suits.

JASON: Really?

Ray: No, not really.

Jason: There are a few people I've had on this show who are still doing radio. One was Steve Allen, as we've already mentioned, and another was one of your fellow New Yorkers, Jackson Beck. He talked about how lonely it is now because, for nearly everything he does now, he is alone in the studio. He used to work with casts of as many as twenty, plus the crew in the control room.

Bob: That's true. He was on a tremendous number of shows. I agree with his theory about being alone. He was on a lot of those old dramatic shows.

Jason: There's still quite a nucleus of talent in New York City from the old radio days. Not as many as there used to be. Many have gone to the West Coast, but Arnold Stang is still there.

Bob: I see him quite frequently. He works close to where I live. I run into him in my neighborhood. Henry is still in our city...Henry Morgan. He's doing a lot of commercials.

Jason: Jackson is still in New York City as well. Henry is someone who can probably match you on the ad-lib, one of the few.

Bob: Of course. He was the first.

Jason: When I caught up with Steve Allen, he was also in New York. He does his show most of the time from there, although he does live in California. Let's talk a little about some of the things you did on your shows, some of the phony ads you made up and still do. Things like "The Little Jim Dandy Burglary Kit" or "The Home Surgery Kit."

Bob: We've done so many. It's like anybody taking out any episode gathering dust. We've done hundreds of those. We always created our own fictitious sponsors so that it had the appearance of being a commercial show, just to make us feel better, I guess. The commercials were very entertaining. We kind of pioneered in those early days of humorous commercials with the Piels Brothers. Those began in the fifties. They won national awards for TV and radio spots when they were only aired in New York and Connecticut. It was really a breakthrough. Everything had been very serious until then. Bert and Harry put kind of a light touch to commercials that people went for, for ten years or more.

Jason: I've seen some of those, not on television, on film.

Bob: The TV things were great. They were animated.

Jason: Have you done any cartoon work? I know you must have.

Bob: Not as much as you'd think. We did a couple of things. Four or five years ago we did some of the voices in Johnny Hart's comic strip *B.C.* I think that was a Christmas show they did in Toronto. Then, we did another one just a couple of years ago, which hasn't been seen in the States, yet. We were on in Canada as long as we were on the radio here, before Public Radio. They used to buy our syndicated material. So we were known as much in Canada as we were in the United States, a long time.

Jason: Was that commercial radio in Canada?

Bob: It was both, but it was a commercial network we were on.

JASON: They have both systems there.

BOB: We went to London a couple of years ago and were guests on a big variety show there, which was quite an experience. We were concerned about how we'd 'go over' in England. We'd been told by a number of people that our kind of thing was something they'd really appreciate. Their reaction was very good. We had a wonderful visit over there. It was exciting to be on a show from London.

JASON: You might almost compare your style to *The Goon Show*.

BOB: They were a little more slapstick than we are. I know what *The Goon Shows* were, and I've heard some of them. I think they're farther out than we ever got. We try to walk a narrow line between reality and fantasy. We were pretty close to real people. Wally Ballou would do an interview like something we'd heard somebody do at some time for real. Most of the things we do are close to reality, but just a hair off.

JASON: I think we can relate any of the characters, you've done, to somebody we've actually heard or seen on radio, or on television, or on film somewhere, just a bit exaggerated.

BOB: Right, Barry Campbell, for instance, is everybody's pompous actor who hasn't had a hit for years, but thinks every show is a big success.

JASON: And he's usually at liberty, as the expression goes.

BOB: Oh, yeah!

JASON: I think the funniest thing in comedy is real life.

BOB: That's what satire is, poking fun at something or somebody. It's not the easiest kind of humor, but if you can think that way, it's a fun kind of humor.

JASON: I think it's the funniest kind of humor there is.

BOB: We do, too.

JASON: I talk with people from most of the different areas of show business. I can't think of many of them that you haven't done a takeoff on at one time or another.

BOB: I guess we've done most of them.

JASON: Of all the characters you've done, do you have a favorite?

BOB: That's hard to say because we like them all. We've used some of them more than others because they fit in, like Wally Ballou or Webley Webster. We probably lean on those two and Mary Magoon more than others.

JASON: Those three can fit almost any situation, but there were others who were more specific. Biff Burns was used a lot for sports interviews.

BOB: And the clichés that have become so much of sports reporting.

****

BOB/BIFF: This is Biff Burns. Today we're going to chat with a grizzled veteran of some twenty years in the game, who's finally retiring. I'm referring to Stuffy Hodges. Stuffy, how are you feeling?

RAY/STUFFY: I feel pretty sad naturally, this being my last game—pretty sad.

BOB/BIFF: Well, I guess that's a reasonable feeling. You can't complain. Over the years, the game has been pretty good to you.

RAY/STUFFY: Not as good to me as some of these young punks who are coming along.

BOB/BIFF: There's a note of rancor there. What do you mean?

RAY/STUFFY: I don't know. This game passed me by somewhere. When I first came up, the game was everything. Sure you got paid for it, but now, it's the big bonus, the big salaries, the big homes, the big cars, the beautiful wives, making TV commercials and movies, and sleeping late in the morning.

BOB/BIFF: Looks like you went wrong somewhere along the line, doesn't it?

RAY/STUFFY: Like I say, the game's passed me by somewhere, I don't know. Now they have these little radios going in the locker room all the way up. They're playing a bunch of noise. I don't understand that music. Whatever happened to Kate Smith and Pat Boone? Those guys sang a song.

BOB/BIFF: It's good to see you've maintained your sense of humor.

RAY/STUFFY: You have to.

BOB/BIFF: In fact, Stuffy, you've got a pretty good reputation around the sports banquet circuit as a real great guy when it comes to telling a sport's story. Would you give us one of those baseball anecdotes of yours?

RAY/STUFFY: Sure, I'll always remember the first time I came up to bat in the big leagues. I was just a kid. They had this big left-hander out there on the hill that day—remember him?

BOB/BIFF: I think I do, yeah.

RAY/STUFFY: He was throwing real smoke that day, see. I couldn't see his pitches at all. So the third strike went by me. The umpire says, "Yer out!" I was young and nervous and everything. I took my bat and threw it straight up in the air. So the umpire took off his mask and he said to me, "Young man"—I was a young man then—"Young man, if that bat comes down, you're out of the game." These kids don't have jokes and anecdotes like that. Their idea of a joke is what they've been doing to me lately. They loosen the spikes on my shoes so I run wobbly, you know? Then they put ice cubes down in my glove and they put cheese in the sweatband of my cap. Took me 'til August to track that down.

BOB/BIFF: I don't want to change the subject, but you know you've been known through the years as someone who likes to burn the light at all hours, day and night. You haven't taken too much care of your diet and yet you're still in pretty good shape physically, Stuffy. How do you account for that?

RAY/STUFFY: Well, I wouldn't put too much stock in what you say there. You see, the worst thing that ever happened to the game was this here AstroTurf. It's like playing the game on a billiard table. Your infielder is about to make a play, the ball takes these crazy hops, jumps up and hits him in the clavicle. You still gotta make a play. You better make that play. You don't make that play and you're not gonna win this game. It goes for both teams—regardless.

BOB/BIFF: Stuffy, you think they're gonna retire your number now?

RAY/STUFFY: Nah, they got some other young punk wearing it now.

BOB/BIFF: I see the mayor and Mickey Mantle and George Jessel coming into the dugout now for the ceremony, so I'm gonna say thanks for talking to me. Lots of luck. We'll see you around, Stuffy.

****

JASON: It's gotten so that you can almost predict what's coming next on any sportscast.

BOB: That's right. Most of them try to keep away from it as much as they can. They're more conscious that people listen for those things, so they try not to do them.

JASON: I think everyone has somewhere in their speech pattern, some expression that they wish they didn't use, but it's hard to get it out of their vernacular. These are things that become cliché, either with the person saying them, or just in general. It's also how some of those expressions get started.

BOB: That's true, I imagine. *I imagine*, is one that I don't like, but I just said it, didn't I?

****

We talked about Wally Ballou, Charles the Poet, Mary Magoon, Biff Burns and Webley Webster, but there were many, many more. Bob added Tex Blaisdell—a singing cowboy, Johnny Braddock—an obnoxious sportscaster and Gore—a Boris Karloff sound alike, just to mention a few. Ray?—Steve Bosco—another sportscaster, Dean Armstead—a farm reporter and all of the feminine parts. The two of them accounted for a virtual cast of thousands.

During our talk, about 3/4s of the way through, unbeknownst to me, Ray had to leave for a prior commitment. Since we were talking over a thousand mile gap, I could not see what was happening; however, being the showman that he was, Bob carried on...doing both voices. I found that out when Bob told me after it was all over. It just proved once more how flexible those two gentlemen could be.

The duo was broken up in 1990 by Ray's unfortunate demise, but Bob continued to work alone through all of the years after that, quite successfully, I might add. Their style, because they did it so well, never got old.

Now I must say a fond farewell to those two kings of subtle jocularity, with their own traditional sign off, "Write if you get work" and "Hang by your thumbs." Obviously, I don't recommend the second option.

Act VI:
Wild, Wild West

Westerns are a form of entertainment that has always been popular throughout the years in all forms of media, whether they are on radio, television, or the big screen.

We have had many movie classics such as *Shane* with Alan Ladd and Jack Palance, or *High Noon* with Gary Cooper and Grace Kelly, or perhaps *Bad Day at Black Rock*, in more modern settings, with Spencer Tracy. We might even think of Clint Eastwood's spaghetti westerns. Television gave us many examples of the genre, including the more recent *Bonanza* and *Maverick*, and on radio there were many more. There were cowboys for kids (*Red Ryder* and *Tom Mix*), singing cowboys (Gene Autry and Roy Rogers), and the more serious, like Jimmy Stewart on *The Six Shooter*, or Raymond Burr on *Fort Laramie*.

It would be foolhardy to try to give credit to all of them on any medium because the list is endless, but there were some that showed up for lengthy runs on both radio and TV and even on film. The most obvious one would be *Gunsmoke*, with ten years on radio and twenty more on the small screen under its belt. Another was *Have Gun, Will Travel*. It enjoyed only two seasons on radio, because radio as we knew it, was dying at that time, but it continued for six years on television.

My point in all this is to introduce two gentlemen who had a big hand in the success of both of those series. Each was a star on one and a featured player on the other. If you are at all into media history you may know who I am talking about, so let us get right into it.

ACT VI:
SCENE ONE
NOT JUST A COWBOY

We come to a man of many talents. He was an actor in diverse roles, a producer, a writer, and in his early days, an animation artist. I might also mention that he was a professional musician. We often remember him as Paladin on the radio version of *Have Gun, Will Travel* and as a bit player on radio's *Gunsmoke*, but his abilities far surpassed those two classic shows. As a matter of fact, he did so much, that I asked him to be my guest on *Life in the Past Lane* on two separate occasions, once to discuss mostly radio and a second time to talk about his television and movie credits, of which there were many.

His name was John Dehner. I was pleased to speak with him on June 2, 1986 and again on May 18, 1987. What I present here is a compilation of both interviews.

****

JASON: John, you were born in New York, but your radio career began in Los Angeles according to my information. How did that all come about?

JOHN: It was quite convoluted. I was born in Staten Island, New York, as you said. Then I lived in Europe for many years. I got my early education in Norway and Paris. I came back and finished my high school in New York. I did a lot of high school drama. Then I went to the University of California and did a lot of drama there with the California

Experimental Theatre at the University. Then I had an offer to join an acting group back in New York. It seemed like a good idea so I went back to New York in 1935 and joined The New York Troupe, which is what it was called. It was run by Andrius Jilinsky who had come over in 1933 with a group of actors from the Moscow Arts Theatre, including Michael Chekhov. In thirty-five I was still studying. In thirty-seven we opened on Broadway in a story by Strindberg called *The Bridal Crown*, which was a total disaster. That was in the depth of the depression, by the way, and oh, boy that was something. I'd never seen such agony and grinding poverty in all my life, but fortunately, I was a young fellow. I was able to take it. It was an incredible experience for the whole nation to go through. People who had had fine jobs, who were well off and pillars of the community, were suddenly reduced to absolute zero. The thing that people forget is that zero is really zero. We had people from our community in upstate New York, Hastings-on-Hudson, who sometimes could be found selling apples in New York City just to make a nickel here and a nickel there. It was disastrous. Somehow we managed to survive. From New York, I went, in thirty-nine, to California. I had had enough of the hand-to-mouth existence in the east, where I had done quite a few things, but still, the money was so poor, that I felt the need to move to a place where I could work regularly and, quote—"EAT"—unquote. So I went to California and tried out as an artist at Disney Studios. I passed the test. See, I trained to become an artist over my high school years, because my father was one. So, when I came to California, I went to work at Disney Studios in the animation department and worked my way up from what they call "In-Betweening" to assistant animator under Eric

Larson. I worked on *Bambi, Fantasia,* and innumerable Mickey Mouse and Donald Duck shorts. My first live action job at Disney, was a thing called *The Reluctant Dragon*. That was Disney's first effort at making a movie combining animation and live acting. I played an animator in the thing, and you'll never guess who the hero was, at a time before he became the outstanding superstar that he did become. That was Alan Ladd. Maybe the dragon out-showed him, but he was the live action star. He was just a feature player then. He still hadn't made *This Gun for Hire*. That was the one that propelled him to stardom. Anyway, that was my beginning. From there I went into the army. After the army, I didn't want to go back to Disney, because I found it to be too confining for me. That's when I wound up on radio. I was an announcer at KFAC, a music station. That was 1942.

JASON: When we think about radio and John Dehner, the first thing that often comes to mind is 'westerns,' because you did so many of them, but in reality, you did so much more, including kids shows like *Buster Brown;* and *Romance*, which was a dramatic anthology—a different story every week.

JOHN: *Escape* was another anthology. I did so many, Jason. It's hard to reach back through the years to even the names of the shows I did, but I did them all in LA. I didn't do anything in the east at all—never did.

JASON: You were somewhat involved with one of the soaps with Mercedes McCambridge, *Family Skeleton*, for Carlton E. Morse.

JOHN: I was, but I wasn't there too long. *Suspense* was another one. An actor in those days did everything he could possibly do to keep himself going. It was a lovely period, because what you did, required a tremendous amount of imagination and skill, and you produced a product you could be rather proud of, because you were presenting your audience with material—grist for their imagination, so they could create their own pictures. Everybody was sort of liberated at the time—the actors, the audience, the director—everybody was very free. It was an experience we all cherish.

JASON: You worked a great deal with Norman Macdonnell.

JOHN: Yes, I worked with Norman on *Escape* and *Romance* and a few other shows he directed and produced. I was with him for nine years on *Gunsmoke*, and at the same time, the last two years, I had my own show, *Have Gun, Will Travel*, on which I played Paladin, while Dick Boone was doing the TV series.

JASON: I believe your approach to the role was quite different from Richard Boone's. I think you were a little more down to earth than he was.

JOHN: Yes, well. he was the Capital H-E-R-O. I turned out to be the hero, but my character didn't play that way.

JASON: *Have Gun* was a radio series rising out of the ashes of television.

JOHN: That's not quite right, Jason. The radio version was concurrent with the TV series. I'll tell you what happened. Dick Boone was doing the Paladin part on TV, and CBS decided to do the show on radio. One of the reasons why they went that way was because they thought they had a backlog of *Have Gun, Will Travel* TV scripts that they thought they could adapt to radio. They thought it was all cut and dried. However; they found out in the doing of it, that the structure of the television scripts was not adaptable to radio. So, they had to do fresh and clean scripts, written exclusively for radio. That's really the history of the radio show.

JASON: That's interesting, because most of the literature on subject doesn't say it quite that way, but then, you would know better than anyone else.

JOHN: Well, sure, I was integral to the whole decision. They had a mother lode of scripts—they thought, but they didn't adapt well, so we had to go our own way.

JASON: Here is just a taste of *Have Gun, Will Travel*, a typical opening with Ben Wright playing Hey Boy and John Dehner as Paladin.

****

ANNCR: San Francisco—1875—the Carlton Hotel—Headquarters of a man named Paladin.

HEY BOY: Good morning, Mr. Paladin.

PALADIN: Hello Hey Boy. I didn't expect you to be at the desk this morning.

HEY BOY: Oh, yes sir, desk clerk ask me to stay here while he help butler. Why you up so early?

PALADIN: Couldn't sleep. I thought I'd pick up the newspapers and have breakfast in the dining room.

HEY BOY: Oh, I was coming up to your room when desk clerk returned. Telegram arrive for you—here.

PALADIN: Thank you.

HEY BOY: Newspapers all folded.

PALADIN: Just the San Francisco paper for now, Hey Boy.

HEY BOY: Ok, here is other California paper. Not much interesting news in paper today, Mr. Paladin? Telegram…interesting?

PALADIN: Yeah, very. Do you remember Lola Blackwood?

HEY BOY: Oh, yes sir. Very famous actress when she come to California theatre. Very nice lady, Mr. Paladin. Hey Boy not see her for long time. She coming back?

PALADIN: No, she retired from the theatre about a year ago.

HEY BOY: Oh, that too bad. I did not know. Lovely lady as Miss Blackwood should always be seen by many people. Why she send telegram?

PALADIN: She needs help, wants me to come at once.

HEY BOY: You go?

PALADIN: As soon as I pack. Get me a seat on the next stage to Sacramento.

****

JASON: Am I correct in assuming that your first regular network program was Smilin' Ed McConnell's *Smilin' Ed's Buster Brown Gang*, and if so, what was your role on it?

JOHN: Seriously, Jason that is an amazing statement, to go back that far. It's a compliment to you and your research.

JASON: 1943?

JOHN: Incredible! That could have been my first regular show. What I played were two or three good guys. It was so long ago I can't remember their names. I was a Hindu Prince. I was the nice husband. I was the good guy all the way through. Isn't it amazing that you should bring that up?

JASON: But never Froggy?

JOHN: This is wonderful.

JASON: *Smilin' Ed's Buster Brown Gang*, here's how every show started.

****

Hey kids! You better come running! It's Buster Brown! (Singing) Buster Brown is on the air. The happy case of Buster Brown is on the air. Hello kids! Hello mother! Hello daddy! Hello grandmother! Hello grand daddy! And uncles and nieces and nephews and cousins and brothers and sisters and all. Hello everybody. This is your old buddy Smilin' Ed and all his Buster Brown gang, Squeaky, the Mouse, Grandy, the Talking Piano, Froggy, the Gremlin, here in Hollywood all ready for another good old Saturday whoop'em up.

****

JASON: In 1943 you worked with Norman Macdonnell for the first time, or at least I believe it was the first time, on a series you mentioned called *Romance*.

JOHN: *Romance*, right.

JASON: It was a quality series, as were all of Macdonnell's productions. I believe that was also your first chance to work with some of the other actors you spent a lot of time with on later shows. I'm speaking of Larry Dobkin for one. Ben Wright was another.

JOHN: Yes, Larry and Ben and Harry Bartell, Vic Perrin, Parley Baer—

JASON: Virginia Gregg.

JOHN: Virginia, oh, my, yes. That was the beginning for me of a very warm and lucrative period in my radio life. There were Georgia Ellis and Bill Conrad. We all worked together from 1943 through to the end of radio drama, which was around 1959, wasn't it?

JASON: I'm not sure. *Have Gun* was on until November of 1960, wasn't it? I think the very last dramatic radio show was *Yours Truly, Johnny Dollar*, a show you also did.

JOHN: I was going to say, *Johnny Dollar* was THE END. That was the end of all radio. I think I was the penultimate. *Gunsmoke* was gone and then *Johnny Dollar*. That was it, "El Swan Song."

JASON: That probably would have lasted a lot longer if it wasn't for the era it was in. It was a good show.

JOHN: I think so. What happened for us who were in radio at the time was a great tragedy. The

	management of the networks turned their backs on their own child, which was radio drama and radio comedy, radio broadcasting, as a matter of fact, in favor of news.
JASON:	And game shows.
JOHN:	Right, so at that point we were just devastated because it was not only a source of livelihood, but, as a medium, it was terribly exciting. We had to create with our voices, unseen by the public, vivid images that the audience itself would conjure up in its imagination. It was a very exciting business, believe me.
JASON:	Something I've said many times, as have others before me, everyone got their own impression of what was going on. You could make your own story because you didn't 'see' anything causing you to preconceive images.
JOHN:	Exactly, and it was the image that you formed in your own mind that was so valuable and so vivid, because it was yours.
JASON:	The only thing we had to watch was the green eye on the face of the radio, and we did do just that, for hours on end.
JOHN:	That's true.
JASON:	Before we move on to the movie and television phases of your career, let's talk a little more about your radio credits.
JOHN:	Before any of that I had a series called *Frontier Gentleman*, then a thing called *The Judge*. I was very active until the very, very end when the

powers pulled the plug on radio drama and a whole industry disappeared when the business interests decided they could make more money, cheaper, by not having radio drama, limiting their talent to two or three talk shows and news. What had been a very good effort and an industry, just died, absolutely vanished. There had been any number of people who were very close. We went from *Romance*, to *Escape*, to *Suspense*, and we all sort of worked all of the shows. It was a very close-knit group. It was very warm, and it was clean. You weren't sitting, sweating on a horse in the boondocks somewhere as you would be on television or in the movies. You were in a clean studio, and it was just dandy with a capital "D."

JASON: That's an aspect of radio I never gave much thought to. When working on television or in movies you had to be on location. Radio was much more comfortable all around. It was all locations in one place. Among your credits you can list several detective shows. *Sam Spade* was one. *Phillip Marlowe* was another; and of course the one we spoke of, *Yours Truly, Johnny Dollar*. My point here is to show some of your versatility. In forty-six, we heard you on *The Count of Monte Cristo*. I believe that may have been the first time you worked with some of the principals from *Gunsmoke*—Bill Conrad, Parley Baer and Howard McNear.

JOHN: Parley was a regular on *Monte Cristo*. Carleton Young was the count. I hadn't thought of it that way, but that was where I met a lot of the actors. Howard was marvelous, a wonderful Doc on *Gunsmoke*.

JASON: As long as we're on the subject of *Gunsmoke*, you

	and Larry Dobkin played a terror of two on that show, mostly heavies.
JOHN:	I played a variety on that, bad and good. I did that show for nine straight seasons, even when I was doing *Have Gun, Will Travel. Gunsmoke* was an integral part of my entire radio experience.
JASON:	*Gunsmoke* played a large part in the lives of a long list of actors, as well as for us, the listeners. Here is John Dehner as Doby, at the sight of a new hotel.

****

DOBY:	Howdy Marshall. How's it coming along?
DILLON:	We're coming along fine, Doby.
DOBY:	Of course, it's only a little bitty hotel. It won't last long.
ENOCH:	Doby, I'll eat the goose that fattens on your grave.
DOBY:	Not likely. Anyways, what do you know about the hotel business, Enoch? You won't last a month.
DILLON:	Stop it boys. There's plenty of trade here. Why don't you stop fighting each other?
ENOCH:	You're just scared of a little competition, Doby.
DOBY:	You ain't gonna last too long, Enoch. There's only enough for one man. You shouldn't be pushing into other people's territory.
ENOCH:	You ain't gonna stop me, Doby.
DOBY:	I've tried to stop you, and I'll keep on tryin'.

ENOCH: Marshall, he's threatenin' me. You heard him.

DOBY: I'm gonna fight you, Enoch. I'm gonna fight you all the way. Now you better start stayin' up at night.

ENOCH: That man belongs in jail, Marshall.

DILLON: Doby's a hard one, Enoch. He'll give you a fight, but I don't think he'll do anything illegal.

ENOCH: Oh, you don't, hey? Well, you just wait and see. It's gonna be your fault for not stoppin' him. I ain't gonna let anybody forget it.

****

JASON: *Gunsmoke*, along with *Romance, Escape,* and *Have Gun* were all Macdonnell productions.

JOHN: That's right; Norman was the producer, which is what they called the director in those days. As a matter of fact, he was the one, along with John Meston, who created *Gunsmoke*. Then, when radio collapsed, Norman went to Universal as the producer of the TV show. So, he had a long history with *Gunsmoke*, and it was an excellent show. Tony Ellis worked on *Have Gun, Will Travel* a lot. He was very much a part of *Gunsmoke* and very much a part of *Have Gun*. I had very strong associations with Tony Ellis. We did *The Judge*. I had three series at CBS, three or four, I can't remember now.

JASON: *Frontier Gentleman* was one.

JOHN: *Frontier Gentleman, The Judge, Pursuit,* along with *Have Gun.* I had four network shows, one after the other. Tony Ellis was very important. He was basically a writer, but a very sensitive and wonderful man.

JASON: Three other guys were really important to *Gunsmoke*, at least that's how I felt as a listener. They were Ray Kemper, Bill James, and Tom Hanley, the sound men. The sound effects on that show went a long way toward making it the success that it was.

JOHN: That was another fascinating part of that or any radio show, but these men particularly, were so skilled and such an integral part of the structure of that program. It was an absolute, total delight to work with them. We'd stand in front of our microphones with our scripts and they would produce such intricate sounds, chase sounds, horses, gun fights, burning buildings and so forth—physical fights.

JASON: Or a dog barking two blocks away.

JOHN: A lone dog howling in the wilderness. With our scripts in our hands, we would keep one eye on the sound men and they on us. They were able to guess by our body English what kind of intensity the sound should have. The two were linked very closely together. They were wonderful.

JASON: It's a kind of lost art these days.

JOHN: That's right, but these were extremely creative moments. Good for you. You thought of those guys.

JASON: Let's talk a little about *Escape*. I understand you did some of the writing for those shows.

JOHN: I did, but not a lot. I did some. I had always been interested in writing, and because of my association with Norm, I was able to have an *entrée*. I could submit my scripts. Some of them turned out to be very good. I sold a few to *Escape* and to *Suspense*. Then I gave up writing, because acting took up most of my time, so that was the end of that; however, I enjoyed it very much. We had a particular problem in radio, which was that with a half-hour show, the actual time of the drama would be something like twenty-four or twenty-five minutes. The rest was introduction, formatting and concluding remarks and credits. Then there were some commercials. So we had to produce an entire story in a very short time. This took a lot of compression in the writing. You had to be extremely concise and direct in the way you wrote your scene. Sometimes we would have to cut them down, word by word, line by line, or take out whole paragraphs, which seemed very likely to change the direction of a story. However; these things had to be done. I enjoyed writing *Escape* very much.

JASON: It was an interesting show, well done all the way through, and again, it was the same group of actors, Bill Conrad, Parley Baer, and Raymond Burr worked on quite a few of those, and Elliott Lewis…

JOHN: Elliott wasn't involved with *Escape*.

JASON: Sorry, I was thinking of *Suspense*.

JOHN: As a matter of fact, I worked with Elliott about three or four years ago on radio. He produced a radio series on sort of a network. I think I did six or eight of them.

JASON: Could that have been *Zero Hour*? No, that was more than three years ago.

JOHN: No, this was something else. These were agency shows. I don't know what network picked them up. Here's an amusing thing. You've heard the name Jerry Hausner?

JASON: Yes, I know Jerry. He invited me to go on one of his guided tours of Germany a few weeks ago. Unfortunately, I couldn't go. Germany is where I was born.

JOHN: Well, Jerry was a wit, and we loved him dearly. I hadn't seen Jerry in years, but when we were doing these revivals with Elliott Lewis, the series he was doing not long ago, I remember sitting at a table with a number of older actors, Larry Dobkin, Virginia Gregg, Ben Wright, etc. We were marking our scripts…preparing to rehearse. The door opened and in came Jerry Hausner. He walked up to the table and saw all of us, whom he had known for years and years. Very quietly he said, "My God, it's like looking into an open grave."

JASON: That's a little frightening.

JOHN: No, it was amusing, it really was. Years had passed, and all of the sudden, here we were, all together again.

JASON: We were talking about Norman Macdonnell. Another Norman you worked with was Norman Corwin on *CBS Workshop*. It was a classy show, but didn't stand a chance because of timing more than anything else.

JOHN: It reflects the usual sad commentary on all of our entertainment business. The good things are always the first to be dropped.

JASON: That's true of television as well.

JOHN: Absolutely. Norman Corwin was THE genius of radio. I remember I did a Charles Laughton thing with him. He was wonderful, painstaking.

JASON: The show was *CBS Workshop*. The story was "Hail and Farewell" by Ray Bradbury and the narrator was John Dehner.

****

Saturday was her favorite. She saved tickets and programs of her favorite stars, railroad transfers and such things, tags and tokens of her experience—she saved. The one thing she most enjoyed touching, listening to, looking at, she hadn't saved. John was far out in the middle country, hidden under ground. Nothing remained of him but his high silk hat, his cane and a good suit in the closet, but what she could keep, she kept. Pink flowers crushed among mothballs in black trunks and cut glass dishes from her childhood. The past lived with her. The thing with the children happened in the middle of the summer. Even that day, coming out of the water, the ivy on her front porch, saw the two sprawling girls, lying on her front lawn, enjoying the immense prickling of the grass. At the very moment she was smiling down at them with her yellow masked face. Around the corner, like an elfin band, came an ice cream wagon. The two girls sat up, turning their heads like sunflowers after the sun.

****

JASON: From a very melancholy story to one of high adventure, we take you once more to the *CBS Workshop* for an adaptation of one of the ancient dramas of Japan.

****

JOHN: Have the Samurai, the lords and nobles arrived?

AIDE: Yes, my lord, they have all come.

JOHN: Among them should be a knight in broken armor, carrying a rusted sword and leading his own lean horse. Find him and bring him to me.

AIDE: I tremble and obey your majesty.

NARRATOR: (*Bill Conrad*) He ran without catching his breath. Among the richly clad nobles, he had no trouble finding Sineo.

JOHN: He has come, indeed. Sineo, Lord of Sunno, have you forgotten the priest who once you sheltered from the snow storm and the boy you once called son?

****

JASON: That was from the Noh plays of Japan, a quantum leap from westerns, just another proof of versatility.

JOHN: Oh, gosh yes, yeah. As far as versatility is concerned, so many radio actors were versatile because they were able, with their voices, to produce so many images of the characters they were asked to portray. They were very flexible people. The only thing about radio was that a lot of radio actors were not appropriate or able to break into motion pictures. They didn't have the standard Hollywood physique that the business seemed to demand at the time. We had no Dustin Hoffman, who, let's face it, is not the hero image that say, Rock Hudson was. A lot of radio actors didn't fit in, so they were able to fulfill their acting destinies as radio actors, but had a terrible time getting into motion pictures. That is not to say that they were anything but very, very qualified and talented people who probably would have made it had our industry been other than it was. This is really a vague statement I'm making, but I hope I'm making a point that you can see.

JASON: It was a little bit of a reversal of what happened when silent films went to sound. People then may have had the image, but didn't have the voice.

JOHN: There you go, very good. I guess I did make my point. Yes, they had the image, but no voice, while here they had the voice, but no image; however; this was a tragedy. Had things been delayed just a few years, these very people would today, in many cases, be superstars, because the image has changed. I brought up Dustin Hoffman as an example of how he's not the image of a superstar in those days, but my god, look at him now. He's a giant.

JASON: Another example along those lines would be Woody Allen. Comedy or drama, he's not a hero image.

JOHN: Woody is another one. But, that is the way it was then, and nothing could be done about it. I just feel very, very sorry that the radio brass kicked radio drama off the air and turned their backs on it, like on their own child, because, had it just hung around, oh my, what we could have produced. As a matter of fact, Jason, and this is interesting— since I'm rambling here. Our old show, *Have Gun, Will Travel* had been scheduled to be picked up for the following season. What made that exciting for all of us was that at that time stereo was beginning to be used and the public was just becoming aware of stereo and what it meant, the power of sound coming from all directions. Our whole series, our whole show was going to be done in stereo the following season. It would have been absolutely tremendous. Imagine a man on horseback coming into town or just riding through town in the dead of the night. You hear the sound of the hooves along the hard packed road in stereo and just expand that to all sorts of situations. This would have been the most exciting thing in the world at that time.

JASON: Ricocheting bullets and the like. A lot of value there.

JOHN: But, what the heck, I went on to what I really wanted to do in the first place, which was become a movie actor. That was my main goal.

JASON: You certainly did have the physique and image for movies. I was watching one the other night, *The Left Handed Gun* with Paul Newman. You played Pat Garret.

JOHN: That was a good show. Fortunately, I seemed to fit into the pattern of what was required of an actor physically at the time. I was tall. I was lean. I wore a black hat well, and I rode a horse well. So, I managed to squeeze into the movie business by way of the western. They, too, were mostly eliminated as a genre. Anyway, I became a movie actor, and I've managed to do pretty well. Now I live up in Sutter Creek, and I work whenever I feel like it, or when they want me, and it's something I agree I'd like to do.

JASON: I saw one of your more recent films not long ago called *The Creator*, which, to me was not a very good movie, but I thought you had a good part in it. The gray hair is there, but that comes with time.

JOHN: Listen, I'm no spring chicken no mo. I loved *Creator*, making it. It was an absolute delight. Peter O'Toole was wonderful to work with and the director, Ivan Passer, was absolutely marvelous. What happened to that picture I know, but I won't tell. There were certain aspects to it that made it extremely tough to do. It could have been better.

JASON: I want to go back a ways to a film I remember well, and a man who had been gone from the scene for quite a while at that time, Stewart Granger. It was *Scaramouche*.

JOHN: Oh, my gosh, yes, *Scaramouche* and Stewart Granger. I played the greatest fencer in all of France. That was a very interesting thing because I played this character who was a fencing instructor, famous teacher—famous swordsman. The physical part had already been filmed. They had used a Belgian, a fencer by the name of Jean Heremans, who had one of the most magnificent noses any human being could be blessed with. They wanted to use him because of his physique and his face, but he couldn't act. So, they brought me in, and I had to have my entire face redone to match his, so that I could play the acting part that he was unable to do. He couldn't even speak the language. So, anyway, that's how I got the part. I worked with Stewart on that. I must say, it was quite successful.

JASON: The first time that story was filmed back in 1922 with Ramon Novarro, it didn't matter what language they were speaking. It was silent.

JOHN: Of course, right. They weren't able to speak at all. They looked good. They could respond to the music that was played in the background while they were shooting their love scenes—oh, boy!

JASON: I want to jump over to TV for a moment. There was a show you did regularly called *The Virginian*. Many of those were written by True Boardman, who told me they were not really westerns. Rather, they were good stories set in a western location.

JOHN: I guess that's true, however, they were westerns. There is no question about that. He approaches his work with a certain parochial view, and I approach mine; but, you can't deny the fact that it took place out west, and we rode horses, and we shot six guns. We did a lot of things that could only be done in the west. In his way, he could be right.

JASON: His theory was that any story could have been converted to a story taking place elsewhere and at a different time. His point was that the themes of all stories are basically the same and just need to be altered to fit a format.

JOHN: Absolutely. I was under contract to Warner's in the early '60s. They had a raft of "Who-Done-Its," gumshoes, detectives, etc., etc., that they were producing, and they actually had a policy that if one producer didn't like a certain script that was submitted to him, they'd say "That's all right," and give it to someone else. They'd turn it over to another producer and change the names.

JASON: You did your share of comedy through the years. I'm thinking of one now called *Temperature's Rising* with Cleavon Little.

JOHN: Cleavon Little—yes. That was actually Paul Lynde's show. There were so many of them that were on for a season, a season and a half and then were off. It was a lot of fun to do. I did *Baileys of Balboa* with Paul Ford. That was a total delight, and I did *The Doris Day Show*. I was her boss for two years on that. That, too, was an awful lot of fun. Yes, I did a lot of comedy, which was rather surprising because, from a western heavy to comedy is quite a jump. I don't know if I have ever really fulfilled any one thing in my life. I've done a lot of things, but I've enjoyed them all.

JASON: The reason I brought up *Temperature's Rising* is that you worked there with a man we talked about earlier on it, a good friend of yours and mine, Jerry Hausner.

JOHN: Oh, yeah, Jerry. Jerry was one of our—I don't know—He was a special person. He had a great sense of humor. He always sparked things whenever he came in to do a radio show. When we were doing those newer things with Elliott Lewis, in the middle of a scene, a very serious scene, he would chirp like a cricket. We'd all wonder, where did the cricket come from? It would practically break up a rehearsal because we couldn't find it. Jerry would be sitting at the table, reading a newspaper, waiting for his cue. He was unique.

JASON: Walter Tetley was known for doing things like that, but Walter worked mostly in comedy. I can imagine the effect it could have if you were doing serious drama and heard something like that.

JOHN: Oh, yeah, crazy. I never worked with Walter, never met him, but he was a positive person, a fixture on radio, no doubt about it.

JASON:	One more TV show, *The Roaring Twenties* with Dorothy Provine. You played a reporter.
JOHN:	Duke Williams. That was the character. That was a property of Warner Brothers. It was a very interesting moment for me because years before, in 1947, I was news editor for KFWB, which was owned by Warner Brothers. I was also a news commentator at the time. I did a broadcast wherein I defended, or spoke favorably about, the Fair Employment Practices Commission, that was being debated in the state legislature at the time. It created a tremendous outcry among certain forces that didn't want to have anything as liberal as fair employment on the statutes. So I stuck my neck out one night in defense of the thing. Low and behold, I was fired the next morning by none other than Jack Warner, who didn't like what I had to say. That was forty-seven. By 1960 it was many years since I had dropped the news business and gone into acting, motion pictures, television, and so forth. Warner Brothers wanted to add this character Duke Williams in *The Roaring Twenties*. It was right up my alley. I liked those kinds of flamboyant characters, so I said sure. We negotiated, signed a contract, and who hired me? After all those years it was the same man who had fired me, Jack Warner. He never realized who I was. He didn't know I was the same man he canned so many years before. It was sort of ironic that I got it all back. I was signed to a seven-year contract at Warner Brothers. Jack Warner looked at me when we met and said, "Glad to meet you. Now you're going to make movies for us, huh?" He patted me on the back, and we went our separate ways. I stayed there for a while.
JASON:	Could that have been before 1960. *Left Handed Gun* was a Warner film.

JOHN: I did that in fifty-eight. No, my statement is quite accurate.

JASON: That was prior to the contract then?

JOHN: *Left Handed Gun* was free-lance. Then I was put under contract when I did *Roaring Twenties*. I've been under contract innumerable times, but I've basically been a free-lance actor most of my life. You know, as an actor, you're always unemployed.

JASON: Between jobs.

JOHN: "At liberty" as we used to say back in those days.

JASON: So what's on the horizon for John Dehner right now?

JOHN: I just finished the sequel to *Winds of War*. You've no doubt seen that mini-series by Herman Wouk. I played the part of admiral Ernest King, who was the commander in chief of the U. S. Navy at the time. This is a sequel we did four years after *Winds of War* called *War and Remembrance*, the second of the two Wouk novels. I play the same character.

JASON: How many of the same people were in both series?

JOHN: Ali MacGraw isn't in it. Jane Seymour did her part. There were a few changes, but it's mostly the same cast. Bob Mitchum is still with us and John Houseman, among others. It's going to be a blockbuster. So far as I can determine now, they have spent over $100,000,000 on it. They haven't finished it yet. They're supposed to finish shooting in October, and they say it will be released next April or May.

ACT VI: SCENE ONE: NOT JUST A COWBOY | 255

JASON: So, all things considered, you're keeping busy.

JOHN: Yes, you can say that John Dehner is a very happy man living in the mother lode country of California, which is the gold country, in a little town called Sutter Creek. I have a lovely home on ten acres of land. Right now, I'm building a stone wall. I'm still working. My last film was a big one in 1985 called *Jagged Edge* with Jeff Bridges and Glenn Close. The one prior to that was *Creator* with Peter O'Toole in 1984. I just turned down a show last week. I didn't like the part, which means I'm still working. I live about two hours from San Francisco, an hour from Sacramento, six hours by driving or an hour by plane from Los Angeles, so I'm well located, but out of the smog and out of the rat race. I'm enjoying myself immensely.

****

As we have noted, John Dehner did a wide variety of work in many genres. We must also remember that, whether radio, television or in the movies, he often tended to return to the western formats that had done so well for him throughout his career. On TV he was a frequent guest on such shows as *Wild, Wild West*, *Maverick* and *The Adventures of Kit Carson*, just to mention a few. Some of his movies other than *Left Handed Gun* were *Support Your Local Gunfighter* with James Garner, *The Fastest Gun Alive* with Glenn Ford and *Apache* with Burt Lancaster.

All things considered, he was Mr. Versatility. While he was often cast as a 'heavy,' he could handle comedy roles with aplomb.

We lost him to diabetes and emphysema in 1992.

I would like to note that in a later conversation, he told me that he did complete the stone wall he talked about, quite a feat for a man his age at the time.

Act VI:
Scene Two
From the Circus to the Plains

Parley Baer tells what it was like to be Chester Proudfoot. This is the first personality, in fact, the only one I have spoken with, who began his career in the circus. While performing there, he met his wife who was with him for fifty-four years until her death in 2000. I will not go into detail about this here, because he will explain it himself.

Perhaps his most memorable role on radio was that of Chester Proudfoot on the audio version of *Gunsmoke*. He did much, much more than that through the years. His name was Parley Baer.

On March 10, 1986 we chatted at length about these and other events in his long acting life that went from 1940 until 1997.

Let's listen in.

****

JASON: Parley, before we get to your media career, let me ask you about a nerve-wracking job you had before your radio days. John Dehner told me you were once a lion tamer.

PARLEY: Long ago I worked an act. I had an act for five or six years. Sometimes it wasn't as nerve wracking as radio and motion pictures. Let me tell you that.

JASON: You know, Red Skelton, at one time, wanted to be a lion tamer until he witnessed a tragic incident. Did you used to worry about that?

PARLEY: The danger was ever present, but so is it when you cross a street. I was lucky. The only scar I have was put on me by a six month old cub. I had a shoulder dislocated a couple of times and I had a jacket ripped off me once. As I said, I was very lucky. I never really got banged up.

JASON: I would guess that those big cats are more unpredictable when they are young.

PARLEY: If they're young, you can't lean on them too heavily, because they don't retain like an older cat. Then, when they start to get old, they become grouchy and cranky, and after an animal has reached seventeen or eighteen, they don't move well. If you try to speed them up, they fight it. Not too long ago I saw a young person trying to help an older lady across the street. She said, "Don't drag me! Don't jerk on me that way." I think that's the way it is with an older animal. You don't make a horse run when he reaches a certain age. You're solicitous of your dog when he reaches a ripe old age. You help him in and out of your car; make sure his water is in a shady place and all that.

JASON: You also have the circus to thank for your wife, Ernestine.

PARLEY: That's true. She was an aerialist and a bareback rider when we met. She's put up with me ever since, almost fifty years so far.

JASON: Which puts to rest the story that Hollywood marriages don't ever last. Let's talk a little about radio. What got you into the field of audio entertaining?

PARLEY: I came along at a time when the stage was ebbing.

I was born in Salt Lake City. I did my first professional radio show in 1933 at KSL in Salt Lake City. I was on the staff there. I also freelanced there. One time, for a period of two years, I was doing twenty-two shows a week and writing eleven of them. Then, World War II came along. After the war, I decided to move to California. I moved here in 1947.

JASON: Most everyone I've talked with over time has had some basic training, so to speak, doing soaps. You must have done some of those, too.

PARLEY: Not too many. About the only soap I did was an occasional shot on *Aunt Mary*. Then Mercedes McCambridge had a soap called *Family Skeleton*. I did that, and then, I did what would have been classified as a nighttime soap called *Defense Attorney*. Mercedes was married to Fletcher Markle. She was a stickler for quality. Once on *Defense Attorney*, she came to rehearse and she didn't think Fletcher's script was a good one. She refused to do it. So he fixed it up and brought her a new one. Another man who was like that was Jerry Devine from *This is Your FBI*. It was always a pleasure to do his shows.

JASON: The only reason I remember *Family Skeleton* at all is because one of my recent guests was Carlton E. Morse. He wrote that for Mercedes.

PARLEY: I did some of those. Not a great many.

JASON: For most of your career you played character parts. Does it seem like there's more flexibility doing that? Is it more fun to play character parts than leading roles?

PARLEY: It is for me, even on the stage. As a young man, I was playing older men's parts. You know, some of us are leading men, and some are not. There are very few of us who are Errol Flynn. I have never wanted to do, *per se*, romantic leads. I've had character leads on both radio and television. I preferred character parts because, let's face it, I have a character face and a character body. I'm not a leading man now, and I never was.

JASON: It seems to me that it's usually the people who do the character parts who are the best remembered, even though we don't always remember then specifically by name.

PARLEY: It has an advantage. The survival rate is higher.

JASON: You played on most of the really well-produced series and anthologies during the '40s and '50s. There was a large group of actors that almost became a traveling repertory company. I'm thinking of people like Bill Conrad, John Dehner, Larry Dobkin, Vic Perrin, and so on.

PARLEY: Virginia Gregg could be added to that list.

JASON: And Harry Bartell and Jeanette Nolan.

PARLEY: John McIntire.

JASON: I can pick up almost any tape of any show from that period and, at least one, often several—'you' are listed in the credits. Here is an example from an episode of *Yours Truly; Johnny Dollar* with Bob Bailey called "The Cask of Death Matter."

****

BOB: I drove to the little town of Kirkwood, Nevada, from which a Mr. Charles Moody had disappeared just about a month ago. I stopped to make inquiries at the general store.

PARLEY: (saying goodbye to a customer). Thank you Miss Beachem. I'll see you next week.

BOB: Now, as you were saying Mr. Hurley—

PARLEY: Yeah, Mr. Dollar, I certainly hope Mr. Moody shows up again. Fine man! Fine man! Used to come down to the store for a quiet game of checkers now and then.

BOB: And—aah—the police have no idea where he might have gone, or why?

PARLEY: Yeah, well, I guess I'm about the only police we have in Kirkwood. Course, I notified the State Police, and I assume they're still lookin' for him.

BOB: Just—what happened, Mr. Hurley?

PARLEY: Just took the bus into Philadelphia one day and, well, that's the last we heard of him.

BOB: Do you know anything about the beneficiary of his insurance? According to my list—

PARLEY: It's a nephew, Mr. Dollar.

BOB: Yeah, Charles Woody—Lives out in California.

PARLEY: Mr. Moody always felt that he was the most deserving of his relatives.

BOB: Left him everything, huh?

PARLEY: Well, the insurance and his money yes. I know, because I'm the only lawyer here in Kirkwood, and I made out a will for him.

BOB: You say, just the money?

PARLEY: Except for his wine cellar, all of his property will go to the town.

BOB: Wine cellar?

PARLEY: Yeah, if Mr. Moody doesn't come back, or if he's proved to be dead, all his wine will go to a man in Philadelphia. Had themselves a sort of gourmet club, I guess you'd call it.

BOB: I see. Now, tell me—

PARLEY: You know, I kinda wish he'd willed me that wine cellar. You should see the collection he has there from all over the world. German wines and French—

BOB: Is there anything else you can tell me to help me find him? How about his friends?

PARLEY: Everybody was Mr. Moody's friend, Mr. Dollar.

****

JASON: There were others in that group that we didn't mention. Frank Nelson was one----

PARLEY: Hans Conried was another name, Sam and Jack Edwards and Willard Waterman.

JOHN: Will Waterman was a recent guest on this show.

PARLEY: Oh, that's good. I think the first network show that I did, he was on it, too, *The Whistler*. Then we did a series called *Those Websters*. I did Billy Idleson's father. The name Will Waterman conjures up a lot of happy memories.

JASON: He spoke well of you as well. Among your dramatic credits is the *CBS Radio Workshop*. You appeared on several of those. I recall hearing you on Aldous Huxley's *Brave New World*. There were so many different characters on it; it's hard to tell which ones you were. You may not remember either, after so long, but that was a classic broadcast.

PARLEY: It was a wonderful thing to do. NBC had a comparable show called *NBC University Theatre of the Air*, which presented adaptations of classic novels. They did a dramatization of "A Passage to India" and some of the Hilton books. I was blessed. I was very fortunate. I did *Hallmark Playhouse* when James Hilton was the original host. They didn't do plays. They also did dramatized novels, current best sellers—as well as some of the classics. When James Hilton left the show, Lionel Barrymore became the permanent host and sometimes also starred in them. He was another man I revered—worshiped for many years. I was very grateful to him. It was part of the era when I did many, many shows. It was a rewarding time, believe me.

JASON: Here's just a small sample of the type of thing that was done on the *CBS Radio Workshop*. This is from "Brave New World." The first speaker is Mr. Huxley.

****

HUXLEY: The year is A.F. 632—632 years after Ford. We are inside the London hatchery and conditioning center. This is the fertilization room, an enormous laboratory where the temperature is never allowed to fall below ninety-eight point six. Here comes the director of hatcheries and conditioning in person with some of his students.

DIRECTOR: Tomorrow you will be settling down to serious work. Today, I just want to give you a general idea of things. These are the incubators. Come on, boys! Now, here we immerse the eggs into a bouillon containing free-swimming spermatozoa. Immersion continues until the eggs are all fertilized. And here is where we bottle the alphas and betas. In short, gentlemen, the perfect process for manufacturing healthy babies. Are there any questions?

STUDENT: Sir, will you explain the Bokanovsky's Process?

DIRECTOR: I'm glad you asked that. Students, take this down. Bokanovsky's process—Where in the olden times, one egg made one embryo, which made one baby. Today, we've improved on all that. Now, the egg will divide into eight to ninety-six buds, and every bud will grow into a perfectly formed embryo and every embryo into a mature baby, making ninety-six humans grow where only one grew before. Progress!!!

STUDENT: But what advantage is it sir, I mean—

DIRECTOR: Oh, my good boy, can't you see? Where in the olden times, nature allowed us to have twins or perhaps triplets or so, today, we can create scores, yes scores of identical individuals. We can manufacture men and women in uniform batches. Think of it! An entire factory staffed with the product of one single egg, ninety-six identical individuals working ninety-six identical machines. At last, society really knows where it stands. Remember, it was our Ford who gave us the concept of the assembly line when he was on earth many centuries ago.

****

JASON: At *CBS Radio Workshop* you also worked with someone to whom most of us concede the title of 'genius.' I'm referring to Norman Corwin. On his series, *26 by Corwin*, a lot of the themes were derived from random ideas. There was a boy looking for his run-over dog on one, the story of a tape recorder on another.

PARLEY: They were original classics. Do you remember a show he did called "The Plot to Overthrow Christmas?"

JASON: Of course I do.

PARLEY: I did that on radio, probably three or four times, and then again for KCET out here. That's the local PBS station. They taped it and made a 1969 TV show out of it—since radio was done. They played that, I guess, for four or five years at holiday time out here. Once more, many of the same people. We had Jeanette Nolan, John Dehner, and also Janet Waldo. I remember I played Simon Legree on it, ten or twelve times altogether.

JASON: That was a real cast. At the station. where I currently work, I produce, direct, cast, and engineer remakes of some of the old scripts from days gone by. "The Plot to Overthrow Christmas" was one of them. It's a lot of fun to do them.

PARLEY: Do you remember a series called the *Sears Radio Theatre*?

JASON: Vincent Price told me about it, but I'm not as familiar with it as I should be. I think it was around seventy-six.

PARLEY: A few years ago. It was a funny thing. Fletcher Markle and Elliott Lewis were two of the directors, and Arch Oboler did some. We came in to do those shows. We sat down, and it was as if the last twenty years had not elapsed. You'd see them three or four times a week, sometimes two or three times a day, as you were flitting from show to show in the old days. If you didn't, you called to see what was the matter, if someone was out of town or ill. We knew when each other's kids had chicken pox. We knew when someone's house had a plumbing problem, or if someone was moving. It was a great, great time. At Christmas we'd get together for parties, things like that. It was a wonderful group. When the *Sears Theatre* went on the air, it was as though those two decades had not passed.

JASON: You probably did some *CBS Mystery Theatre* programs that were also aired recently. A lot of people from the golden years were brought back to do those. Unfortunately, people don't seem to have the attention span to really let anyone make them use their imaginations anymore.

PARLEY: I've said this many times. Radio is the ideal medium for performers. It was referred to by Arch Oboler, or one of those fellows, as "The Theatre of the Mind." If there were ten million people listening, you were giving ten million different performances. It had its own excitement. For *Lux Radio Theatre* or *Hallmark Playhouse* at the Lowes Theatre, now the James Doolittle Theatre—for a long time it was the Vine St. Theatre—every week was an opening night. You got the same butterflies and the same generation of excitement as you did on stage. For many years we dressed for those shows, tuxes and long gowns. Sometimes we got laughs if somebody was playing a prospector leading a burro across the sands of the Great American Desert. It looked ridiculous wearing a tuxedo, so they finally cut that out.

JASON: John Dehner made a good point that I hadn't ever thought about. He said that radio was a really clean medium, because you could be riding a horse in a nice clean air conditioned studio and never get dusty.

PARLEY: Right, we didn't sweat much in those days.

JASON: They did in those earlier days in Chicago. I remember a few stories I've heard from people from that venue.

PARLEY: Back in my days at KSL, air conditioning was an iffy thing. Of course, the poor sound effects men, in the days before taped sounds—sounds were made manually—they had to run through piles of half coconut shells and a plumber's friend for horse's hooves, through the gravel in the fields. Those things were tiring. In those days, if you weren't doing something, you had to get over there and help because two or three men couldn't do it all. You had to have crickets, marching feet and so many other things. It took the combined efforts of everyone who wasn't on mike.

JASON: They were incredible. I particularly remember the three sound men from *Gunsmoke*. They did things that were beyond belief.

PARLEY: They were as dedicated as the actors. They spent many hours on their own. They went out and recorded .22s and .38s and .45s and rifles and shotguns, so if you were shooting a shotgun, you had a shotgun sound. If you were shooting a rifle, you got a rifle sound. They actually recorded those things out of doors for authenticity. They painted pictures with their sounds.

JASON: Let's drop back to the '40s and *The First Nighter*. You worked on many of those.

PARLEY: That was in the early '40s out of Chicago, early and middle '40s. I was overseas nearly four years. My first, *First Nighter* was in late forty-seven, about that time the show moved out here from Chicago. *First Nighter, Those Websters, Lum and Abner,* a lot of those Chicago shows moved out here.

JASON: On a show like *First Nighter*, you played different roles every week. Did that make it more challenging than playing a sustaining character?

PARLEY: Les Tremayne had it first and then Olan Soulé and Barbara Luddy were the permanent leads. It was like a regular stock company, but they were the leads. There were all kinds of parts. One week we'd do comedy, another week drama. We did a whole lot of mysteries. If you were accepted by the director, and you worked well with the company, you could rest assured you would probably do ten or twelve. In those days, the season was thirty-nine weeks. You could be pretty sure of doing at least one third of them. The parts were there.

JASON: Usually, there were summer replacements for most of the shows.

PARLEY: Generally, a dramatic show would replace a dramatic show, a variety show by a variety show, and so forth.

JASON: I'm going to bring up one that I hope you remember. For those who think that television is where all of the new ideas come from, you should tell them about *Granby's Green Acres*.

PARLEY: That was a summer replacement. I've forgotten who it replaced. It had Bea Benaderet, Gale Gordon, Louise Erickson and Rye Pillsbury (later known as Michael Rye). I played Eb, the hired hand. I did a show with Larry King not too long ago, and he played segments from that show. I had almost forgotten about it. *Granby's Green Acres* was, of course, the foundation for TV's *Green Acres*.

JASON: One reason I brought it up was that you played Eb on it. It was the only name that remained the same on TV.

PARLEY: Oh, yeah, I know. He was that long skinny kid. That's right, that's right.

JASON: If I'm not mistaken *Granby's* only ran one summer.

PARLEY: We were on thirteen weeks—that was it.

JASON: It was one of the few summer comedy shows Ransom Sherman didn't do. I'm sure you know Ransom.

PARLEY: For sure. Jay Sommers produced *Granby's* and he later became the head writer and producer of *Petticoat Junction*.

JASON: There again, Bea Benaderet. My guests have talked a lot about Bea. They all said she was a super lady.

PARLEY: A great, great talent.

JASON: *Honest Harold* was the result of some network skullduggery that didn't work. You showed up on that one with Hal Peary.

PARLEY: Hal, and NBC, and Kraft came to a parting of the ways, and he came over to CBS for a few years. The show was *Honest Harold, the Homemaker*. Olan Soulé was on that and Joe Kerns.

JASON: Jane Morgan.

PARLEY: ...and Mary Jane Croft and Gloria Page. She was Harold's wife, a running part.

JASON: What can you tell me about *The Count of Monte Cristo*, with Carleton Young?

PARLEY: Victor Rodman was playing that part and before that, an actor named Ferdinand Gingay. Ferdy died from a heart attack and Vic replaced him. Then Vic got in an accident. This was about forty-nine or fifty. Then Vic died. I played Rene for five years. When Carleton left the show, William Woodson played the Count.

JASON: Some of the others we've discussed showed up there, too—Bill Conrad, John Dehner, Larry Dobkin...

PARLEY: Oh sure, Vic Perrin, Harry Bartell...

JASON: What's interesting is that, even though you know their voices, you can't always tell who's who.

PARLEY: Jaime del Valle directed that when it was on Mutual, and he also directed *Cisco Kid*. We played

	on that quite a bit. Somebody bought it after Harry Lang died. Mel Blanc went on playing Pancho and Jack Mather played Cisco.
JASON:	You still work with Mel these days, don't you?
PARLEY:	Oh yes, quite frequently. We were in Chicago a couple of years ago. They have a big Christmas party there at Leo Burnett, the ad agency. They brought a bunch of us back. Frank Nelson who does Hubert, the Harris Lion for Harris Bank, John Irwin who does the voice of Morris, the Cat, Mel did Sylvester, and I am the voice of Ernie Keebler. All of us went there for the Christmas party. We did bits ala our own characters.
JASON:	You worked with Norman Macdonnell on *Escape*, *Phillip Marlowe* and a few other things. He was, without a doubt, one of the most able directors or producers of radio programming and later, television. In fifty-two, he brought us a show that ran a long time on radio before an even longer time on TV. That show was *Gunsmoke*. Who can forget your voicing of Chester Proudfoot?

****

MATT:	There! Now what's your excuse this time, Chester?
CHESTER:	oo-oo-oo-oh, who?
MATT:	I just took all your men. The game's over.
CHESTER:	Oh now, Mr. Dillon, I don't think checkers is a very good game.
MATT:	What's the matter? Can't you keep your eyes open?

Chester: Oh no, it ain't that. It's them colors. They get kinda bleary, kinda hard to tell the red from the black. You ever notice that?

Matt: Doesn't make much difference to me.

Chester: How's that?

Matt: I wind up with all the checkers anyway.

Chester: Oh, come on now, Mr. Dillon.

****

Parley: Those were ten happy, happy years. The company remained intact. We had two divorces and three births during that tenure. Fortunately there were no deaths. There was Bill Conrad as Matt and the same director, the same assistant director, the same script girl, the same engineers, and the same sound men. And there again, all those same voices we talked about. There were a lot of us. We did two shows for that. We did the show, and they taped it. It played Sunday night with a repeat on the next Saturday morning. We did the first one live, and then they played the tape for the repeat. After a while we started doing it all on tape. We used to do two or three every other Saturday. I did all but five of them. I was overseas doing a picture called *The Young Lions*. We ran into bad weather, but they had recorded ahead for my part, six weeks ahead. We were over there eleven weeks, so there were five shows that I did not do. Bill didn't miss any.

Jason: What was really amazing about *Gunsmoke* was its longevity, considering that it ran into the time when entertainment radio was breathing its last gasps.

Act VI: Scene Two: From the Circus to the Plains

PARLEY: Definitely. It was almost the last big dramatic show that was on radio, something we were all grateful for. When it did go off the air, we were recorded ahead. Bill was doing a picture, I think. We had about four ahead. We didn't know when we were doing our last show. I would have hated to know it was the last time we were going to do it.

JASON: It might have come off quite differently had you known.

PARLEY: You know, there were very few repeats. I can't think of more than three or four that we redid. It was new material, a new show every week. John Meston wrote most of them. Eighty-five per cent of the shows were John's work.

JASON: He continued writing for the television shows, if I'm not mistaken.

PARLEY: They used a lot of our old shows when *Gunsmoke* was a half hour show. They used an awful lot of our half hour radio scripts. They had versions that were tried and proven, so all they had to do was build the sets for them and then play them.

JASON: It's not too hard to expand a thirty minute radio show to an hour on TV.

PARLEY: Right, twice as many commercials. They just had to add twenty or so minutes.

JASON: Speaking of television, you did a bunch of those shows. On *The Addams Family*, you were an insurance agent.

PARLEY: I later played the mayor on that.

JASON: Wasn't that *The Andy Griffith Show*?

PARLEY: I played Mayor Stoner on Andy's show, but also the insurance man and another mayor on *Addams Family*.

JASON: You worked on so many TV shows through the years. Wasn't *The Lucy Show* one of them?

PARLEY: Just the other day I saw an old *Lucy Show* I was on. Over a period of twenty years, I played on a lot of her shows.

JASON: Do you remember doing *The Untouchables*? I thought I spotted you on one of those reruns recently.

PARLEY: I only did two of them.

JASON: Well, I saw one. You are very recognizable. I can't always pick out your voice because you know how to change that.

PARLEY: A guy over at Warner's said to me, "I stopped counting. As near as I can authenticate it, you've done about nine-hundred and forty TV shows. Then I started counting radio. I got up to about eighty-five hundred network shows. After that, I just stopped counting."

JASON: In some ways, television has gotten to be a bit similar to what I called a traveling repertory company on radio.

PARLEY: I suppose that's kind of true now, but not as much. Casting has changed; where some years ago senators, or governors, or what not were always vintage, now they're played by young people. In the old days of radio, you could judge the part you would get, by the director you were working with. One might see you as Eb, the hired hand, while another would see you as a dishonest mayor.

JASON: Age was no factor on radio if you could change your voice. Orson Welles was doing older parts when he was still in his teen years.

PARLEY: It was just what we could do, so we did it.

****

Parley Baer was a true delight. We continued to talk for quite some time after the recorder was turned off. As it turned out, we had something very intriguing in common. For many years, before I got involved in radio, I was a professional pilot. Along the way, I had a chance to do some movie doubling in some flying scenes. One of those movies was *Cash McCall*, starring Jim Garner and Natalie Wood. It also featured Mr. Baer, so in truth, we worked in the same movie, even though the scene structure did not allow us to ever meet.

Parley died in 2002 from complications of several strokes. He was always one of my own personal favorite performers. He always reminded me of the good neighbor I never had. He could be seen in some of the most surprising places on the screen and on television. It was almost like, "Here's a new show, I'll bet Parley's in there somewhere."

ACT VII:
KEEPING US INFORMED

There are so many kinds of news in our world of over saturation. Most of what we see and hear on radio and television is brought to us by people who, at the BBC in Briton, would be called news readers, because that is mostly what they do, read copy. There are fewer and fewer local bylines in our newspapers, due to the advent of so much computer information readily available to just be picked off and copied.

One of the news forms that is still to be noted is investigative reporting, and to some extent, documentaries.

The point I am trying to make is that the news, in general, is not what it used to be or should be.

There was a man who lived a short life, but who developed most of the long-standing techniques for gathering, assembling, and reporting what is going on in the real world. That man was Edward R. Murrow. Since he died in 1965, it is obvious that there was no way to talk with him in 1986, but there was a way to get the inside insights on his life.

On June 15, 1986 I spoke at length with Ann Sperber, author of *Murrow, His Life and Times*. She spent many years putting it together, but the result is well worth her efforts.

****

JASON: Tell me a little about your background and how you got interested enough to spend the long time you did doing research for this book.

ANN: Murrow had been one of my heroes in college. I originally came out of Austria as a very, very small child, just one step ahead of the Nazis. When I was in college and Joe McCarthy was beginning to have a kind of familiar look, Murrow was the man who took him on and really had a great deal to do with his eventual downfall. So naturally, he became my hero. I might also add that I was a government major. I later went into publishing, so these things all came together. Then in 1971—I can give you the year and almost the date—The Lincoln Center was having a retrospective of CBS documentaries. I live in New York. The Lincoln Center is just a couple of blocks from where I live. It was a kind of a down time, if you recall. We were deeply mired in Viet Nam. The voice of attorney general, John Mitchell, was heard in the land, and people were just starting to whisper about those things that later came out under the heading of Watergate. Anyway, I went into this dark little theatre, surrounded mostly by journalism students, wondering if watching Murrow take on McCarthy would have the same impact as it did years ago, and suddenly, I felt it had about ten times the impact. I found this man's conviction absolutely piercing on the screen. It grabbed everybody in that room, but I thought, oh, well, there really hasn't been anyone like him, ever. I got interested, for the first time, in Murrow, the man. When you watch newsmen, newswomen too, you kind of take them for granted. Now, in the later context, I thought I'd really like to know more about this man. My book, in the first instance, was sparked by plain old curiosity.

JASON: You talk about Mr. Murrow and his ability to communicate. The biggest item in his catalogue of talents was the fact that he was an audio-

ACT VII: Keeping Us Informed

communicator. He was descriptive, and he used a narrative style rather than a newspaper style, but before we get into that, I think we should go back to his early life.

ANN: He was a southern boy by birth, born in North Carolina to a farm family. They couldn't make it in those years before the war, so they moved to the Pacific Northwest. His father got a job as the engineer of a little engine hogging logs down a mountain. They were what today would be considered, the working poor. Murrow worked his way through college and eventually ended up in New York as The head of a national student organization.

JASON: When he was in high school in Washington State, he was very well accepted. He was vice president of the student association and valedictorian as well.

ANN: He was one of those very all around people, good grades, good baseball player, played championship basketball, champion debater and yet, and this was always a remarkable thing about him, nobody ever held his success against him. He was one of those people who could be popular, and successful, and liked all at the same time—pretty rare.

JASON: The quote under his picture in his senior yearbook says just that. Quoting from *Love's Labor Lost* it said: *A man in the world's new fashion planted, that has the mint of phrases within his brain.* Who had more phrases within his brain than Ed Murrow?

ANN: That's right and yet, one thing that he really resented all his life was the fact that, in order to raise the money, even to go to the State University, he had to drop out of school. For a young man in a hurry, losing a year was not something that was welcome.

JASON: He worked in a logging camp during that time?

ANN: He went to work as a manual laborer, worked first as an axe man, then worked his way up to surveyor's assistant. It was heavy work and outdoor work. He always liked manual labor, but not as a full time, dawn to dusk occupation, with nothing else in sight. He was always aware that he had come from a part of the country and a society where there was no upward mobility. In his later life, when he became a journalist, he always related best to the people he had come from. He never let his success get the better of him.

JASON: And he always thought of himself as a teacher, rather than as a newsman?

ANN: Oh, I don't think so. I think that's kind of a myth. Murrow was, first of all, reporting the news, not essentially didactic. If you want to say you're teaching people something. the minute you bring them information, you're telling them something they didn't know before—you could say you're teaching them, in that sense. But that's sort of one of the many myths that grew up around Murrow—his being an educator, a teacher, more of a teacher than a newsman. He was a political animal first and last. He was a journalist from his toes up. The jobs that he held, such as being the assistant director of The Institute of International Education, in the early 30s, were all generally political in nature, because they were dealing with the international scene at a time when Hitler and Mussolini were coming to power. He had more to do with assessing the international situation than having to do with education in the ivory tower sense. He loved to teach, in the sense that he wanted to convey information to the American public. He also liked to help younger journalists. He always had an eye out for the next generation. As Charles Kuralt said, as Marvin Kalb said, and many other people, he was remarkably generous in giving of his time and his backing, so in that way you could say he was a teacher in the best sense, but not a teacher in opposition to being a newsman.

JASON: Another thing that seems to have been very important in his life was timing. He was in the right place at the right time on several occasions when it really counted. For instance, when he started out, he was just filling 'dead air' on CBS, which was a fledgling network at that time in 1930—just two years old.

ANN: That's right. He was president of the National Student Federation of America and network radio was very young. They needed to fill that dead air in the afternoons, and so he was in charge of the organization of this sort of interview program that they had once a week. It was probably his first experience at going on the radio. That was in 1930.

JASON: That would have been the *University on the Air.* Is that correct? Or, the *CBS University of the Air*? September 15th is the date you have in your book.

ANN: You really have read it. As an author, I'm delighted.

JASON: We were talking about Murrow's incredible timing in career situations and how he was able to control the outcome in most of them.

ANN: One could say that he did live in stirring times. He did seem to find himself in one crisis after another. To be in London on the eve of World War II when the momentum towards war was picking up speed—to be essentially in charge of the CBS operation when it was so tiny. In 1937 Murrow WAS the European office. He had one sidekick on the continent who happened to be William L. Shirer, whom he hired. Then in March of 1938, when Germany marched into Austria, this was, of course, one of the first signs that the order of things was deteriorating, so CBS set up its first news roundup. There was Murrow at the center of it, setting it all up with Bill Shirer. He always seemed to be on the spot, however, there was another element to that. That is, that he was a good administrator, very creative, and a good journalist. He knew what he was doing. He was a man who could realize, when an opportunity was there, that this was the right time to do the right thing about it.

JASON: This was when? 1938? He then made his first European broadcast, because he had been working behind the scene until then.

ANN: Okay, We take you back to March 12, 1938. German troops have just moved into Austria. Hitler is expected by an eager and admiring Austrian population. The problem was that Murrow, having been an administrator, used to be able to get newspaper reporters to do the reports for CBS. This being a crisis, there were no newspaper people available, so Murrow took a plane from London to Vienna and did the first report himself—simply because he was the only guy there. And so, a great broadcaster was born.

****

ACT VII: KEEPING US INFORMED

This is Edward Murrow speaking from Vienna. It is now nearly 2:30 in the morning and Herr Hitler has not yet arrived. No one seems to know just when he will get here, but most people expect him some time after ten o'clock tomorrow morning. We're planning to give you an eyewitness account of Herr Hitler's entry into Vienna sometime tomorrow. I return you now to America.

****

JASON: It's interesting to note that he said Edward Murrow, the only time I ever heard him not use the R. in the middle.

ANN: It's funny, but every once in a while, broadcasting from London, he simply said Edward Murrow. It was kind of a shocker because we're so used to hearing the R., of course.

JASON: He certainly built up some troops over there in the reporting business by hiring people like Eric Sevareid, Richard C. Hottelet, Charles Collingwood and, of course, Winston Burdett, and many others.

ANN: He was a terrific talent scout. He really had his eyes open and knew instinctively what would make a great broadcast reporter. As a matter of fact, he often had to fight New York in order to get some of the best talent onboard. He had to fight management back in New York when they didn't want William Shirer, and they didn't want Eric Sevareid. You have to remember, these were much younger men, although Bill Shirer had a good newspaper reputation. Murrow knew that New York didn't know what they were getting. All they were concerned with—was the broadcast voice. They didn't have the lovely baritone that Murrow had. New York simply said, "We don't like their voices. We don't want them." Murrow used to tell them he was hiring reporters, not announcers.

JASON: They certainly stood the test of time. They're all still around. I'm not sure about Winston Burdett.

ANN: I believe he is in Italy now. I think he still does some work. You know quite a number of them have gotten to retirement age and beyond. Although, most of them—not Shirer of course, who was four years older than Murrow—some of the others like Charles Collingwood were literally kids. But, he knew these kids were darn good.

JASON: You have some pictures in your book that prove their youth. They do look very, very young, which, of course, they were. Ed Murrow could appoint people to cover locations because he was the head of the European Bureau, but he also did a lot of reporting himself, including some riveting verbal essays from rooftops during the London Blitz.

ANN: The London rooftops were what gave Murrow his real national reputation. This was 1940. America was not yet in the war, but Germany had conquered all of Europe. The only holdout was this little island nation of Briton, just off the coast of France, twenty miles away across the English Channel. London was getting bombarded every night. Hitler was trying to knock out the air force of England, the RAF. London was in flames. Murrow knew that the only way to convey this reality to the American public and let them know what was at stake, was to get up on the rooftop himself while everything was going to hell around him, with a microphone, and report live from the middle of an air raid. From, by the way, the top of the building housing the BBC, which was a prime target that the Germans were trying to knock down every night.

****

This is London. The plane is still very high and it's quite clear that he's not coming in for his bombing run. Earlier this evening we heard a number of bombs go sliding and slithering across the roof to fall several blocks away. Just overhead now—the burst of the anti aircraft fire. Still, the nearby guns are not working. The searchlights now are flashing almost directly overhead. Now you'll hear some bursts nearby in a little moment. There they are. The fire and smoke goes on.

****

JASON: Another place, that he did some reports from on a fairly regular basis, was from airplanes—on bombing raids or parachute drops, all kinds of things like that.

****

Waiting to jump. You can probably hear the snap as they check the lashing on the static line. There they go, you can hear them jump. 3, 4, 5, 6, 7, 8, 9, 10, 11, 12, 13, 14, 15, 16, 17, 18, every man out. I can see the chutes falling down, down. Every man clear. They're dropping just behind, a little bit, near a church, hanging there, great white flakes. Looking so much like khaki dolls hanging beneath green lamp shades.

****

JASON: There was a real classic report that he did. It was

from an airplane, a Lancaster dubbed "D-Dog."

ANN: Actually, it was not directly from the plane. What it was, was a write up of the entire bombing run over Berlin—from before the plane took off, over to Germany and back. What it was like to be in a bomber getting shot at and then coming back. This was something he wrote up almost the minute he left the plane, without pausing for so much as a cup of coffee. It was an absolute classic because he concentrated on the horror of war and did not try to glamorize what was happening.

****

A tremendous blob of yellow light appeared dead ahead, another to the right, another to the left. We're flying straight for them. And then, with no warning at all, D-Dog was filled with an unhealthy white light. I was standing just behind Jock and could see all the seams on the wings. The quiet Scot's voice beamed into my ears, "Steady boys, we've been coned." His slender body lifted half out of the seat as he jammed the control column forward and to the left. We were going down. Jock was wearing woolen gloves with the fingers cut off. I could see his finger nails turn white as he gripped the wheel. And then I was on my knees flat on the deck. He had whipped the Dog back into a climbing turn. The knees should have been strong enough to support me, but they weren't. And the stomach seemed to be in some danger of letting me down too. D-Dog was corkscrewing. As we rolled out on the other side, I began to see what was happening to Berlin. The clouds were gone and the sticks of incendiaries from the preceding waves made the place look like a badly laid out city with the street lights on. The small incendiaries were going down like a fistful of white rice thrown on a piece of black velvet. The cookies—the 4000 pound high explosives, were bursting below like great sunflowers gone mad. And then, as we started down again, still held in the light, I remembered that the Dog still had one of those cookies and a whole basket of incendiaries in her belly. And the light still held us, and I was very frightened. I looked down and the white fires had turned red. They were beginning to merge and spread just like butter does on a hot plate. The bomb doors were opened and then there was a gentle upward thrust under my feet. Then Boz said, "Cookie gone." A few seconds later the incendiaries left and D-Dog seemed lighter and easier and we could breathe. All men would be brave if they could leave their stomachs at home. Our navigator signed off a new course and we were headed for home. I looked on the port beam at the target area. There was a red, sullen, obscene glare. Berlin was a kind of orchestrated hell, a terrible symphony of light and flame.

****

JASON: What a wordsmith he was, "An orchestrated hell," "A symphony of light and flame." I'm sure his description was very apropos.

ANN: Yes, very much so. He also talked about the sheer terror of being up there in the sky, and looking down, and realizing what was happening down there, even though he couldn't see it through the fire. A line in that broadcast said, "Men die in the sky, while others are roasted in their cellars." This was a very different sort of tack from the usual "Whoopee" sort of reporting that was going on at the time, which I think we both remember.

JASON: At the end of the war, Ed Murrow had the misfortune to experience what was going on at Buchenwald.

ANN: As a matter of fact, Charles Collingwood, when I interviewed him, told me about a poker game they'd had the night before. This was, I believe, in April of 1945. Murrow attached himself to Patton's army as a correspondent. They started getting reports from these places called concentration camps where the allied troops were finding the dead and what Murrow called, "The Living Dead." He was maybe the first, certainly one of the first people, inside the infamous camp called Buchenwald, where he actually came across people whom he had known in peace time, whom he didn't recognize anymore.

JASON: I didn't realize that he met people there that he knew.

ANN: Yes, he mentioned in a broadcast, seeing a man stagger up to him in a barracks where people were sleeping five to each wooden bunk. It had been originally built as a stable to house eighty horses. There now were something like 1200 men packed into it. One of the living corpses came up to him and said, "You remember me?" I'm Petr Zenkl, former mayor of Prague." Murrow later said, "I knew him, but I could not recognize him." When he saw some of these bodies, he said he thought he was going to be sick, but he could not do that in front of people who had endured so much themselves. What especially infuriated him, as he said in his broadcast, was all the people on the other side of the barbed wire, well-fed German citizens, calmly plowing their fields—going right past this place where other people were going through hell. It stayed with him for the rest of his life.

JASON: I'm sure it would. I have a very dear friend in

Holland who had been an inmate at one of the other camps, Bergen-Belsen. He had the terrible experience of seeing his whole family die in the gas chamber. He was in there as well, but was one of the few fortunate people who happened to be near the bottom of the pile and somehow managed to survive. To this day, he still wakes up at times screaming. It was not something that could ever be forgotten.

****

Men crowded around, tried to lift me on their shoulders. They were too weak. Many of them could not get out of bed. As I walked to the end of the barracks there was applause from the men too weak to get out of bed. It sounded like the hand clapping of babies. As I walked out into the courtyard a man fell dead. Two others, they must have been over sixty, were crawling toward the latrine. I saw it but will not describe it. In another part of the camp they showed me the children, hundreds of them. Some were only six. One rolled up his sleeve and showed me his number. It was tattooed on his arm. 6030 it was. The others showed me their numbers. They will carry them until they die. The children clung to my hands and stared. We crossed the courtyard. Men kept coming up to speak to me and to touch me. A professor from Poland—a doctor from Vienna—men from all Europe—men from the countries that made America. We proceeded to the small courtyard. There were two rows of bodies stacked up like cordwood. They were thin and very white. Some of the bodies were terribly bruised, though there seemed to be little flesh to bruise. Some had been shot in the head but they bled so little. It appeared that most of the men and boys had died from starvation. They had not been executed, but the manner of death seemed unimportant. Murder had been done at Buchenwald. God alone knows how many men and boys have died there over the last twelve years. I pray you to believe what I have said about Buchenwald. I reported what I saw and heard, but only part of it. For most of it, I have no words. If I've offended you by this rather mild account of Buchenwald, I'm not in the least sorry.

****

JASON: After that horrendous report allow me to move forward to happier times.

****

This is London. Tonight London is a city of song and celebration and thanksgiving. There are fireworks and partying. Air raid shelters are as remote as the counter fighting. The organized killing has ended in Europe. The nations that have suffered and sacrificed have achieved victory. The coming years and months will reveal what will be done with that victory.

****

JASON: With the end of the war, Ed Murrow was taken away from the microphone and set up in New York in an office, which didn't appeal to him.

ANN: He was persuaded to leave the microphone and take the job of Vice President and General Manager of News for CBS. He became a company VP and had a fancy office on a higher floor. He took over the news department and actually did a very good job in a very difficult time, when you had a news department that was geared to war reporting. He had to make a very difficult transition to peace time reporting, just very different kinds of areas.

Also, sponsors were pulling out—sponsors who, throughout the war, paid very handsomely for the privilege of supporting news programs. Now they figured they would return to backing entertainment. News was suddenly an underfunded department. Murrow did an excellent job of it, but, he was still basically a broadcaster. He did not really enjoy what he was doing. He wound up having to fire two of the people with whom he was very close. He just decided it wasn't for him. In September of 1947, he was one of the few people who left the executive floor voluntarily and just went back to being a broadcaster again.

JASON: That's about when he formed the documentary unit and started doing his nightly think pieces.

ANN: You mean the radio documentary unit or *See It Now*?

JASON: No, maybe *Hear It Now*?

ANN: *Hear It Now* was a little later. That came around 1950. I'll tell you something, with all the various documentary units, it's kind of hard keeping them in place. It was for me. I kept on checking from one page to another—do I have the right unit? However, what he went back to in the fall of 1947 were nightly news reports, a fifteen minute news broadcast from 7:45 to eight o'clock in which, as you point out, there was about a five minute commentary at the end of each broadcast after the foreign news.

JASON: That would have been what he often called his think pieces.

ANN: Yes, exactly, and they were very good pieces. When

you read about them now, and read what he had to say about the Hollywood Hearings, and the House Un-American Activities Committee, and all those who practiced McCarthyism before it was known as "McCarthyism." Those were pieces that really kept up spirits in those years.

JASON: A little later he got back into working in the field. He was over in Korea.

****

This is Korea where a war is going on. That's a marine digging a hole in the ground. They dig an awful lot of holes in the ground in Korea.

****

ANN: He was there in the summer of 1950. Just about as soon as the war broke out, and he was able to get his papers cleared and make his arrangements, he was over there covering the war and, by the way, although he had briefly, at least, very much supported the American presence there, after having been there for about ten days, he wondered if we were hurting more than helping. That broadcast was short waved back to New York for taping and playback on the 7:45 news, but they never ran it. It was decided by the upper management to kill the broadcast, but nobody told Murrow who was still in the Far East at the time. He didn't know until he got back to New York that they had, in fact, censored that piece.

JASON: When did he return from Korea?

ANN: He was out in Korea for only a couple of weeks in the summer of 1950. He didn't get back there until late December of 1952. As a matter of fact, for Murrow, having this nightly newscast was a very frustrating thing because he considered himself basically a shoe leather reporter. Everyone looked up to him as a commentator, and he enjoyed writing his think pieces. What you said before about him being in the right place at the right time was mostly because he was essentially a man of action. He liked to be out there on the front. He liked to be covering something. He did not really enjoy being in a New York office or a New York newsroom having to go over other people's wire copy. Given his druthers, he probably would have much rather spent his time running around covering the stories.

JASON: He was able to get some court cases reversed during his career. I'm going to play a piece from the Milo Radulovich case.

ANN: If we're talking about courts, we're really talking about military courts, the military hearing boards, which were a kind of court, although, unfortunately, in those cases, there are no juries. The boards are their own judge and jury. This was a landmark television program that he did on his documentary series *See It Now*. This was 1953. There was a young man, not too far from where you are now, Lieutenant Milo Radulovich, living in Ann Arbor, Michigan, who was going to be dismissed from his job as an Air Force meteorologist because his father read the wrong newspapers and because they didn't like his sister's politics. Murrow and his partner, Fred Friendly, did a program saying, "No matter what the father does, no matter what his sister does or whatever, if we're in a position where judgment can be made because people don't like one's relative's politics, we're in a pretty bad way."

****

We believe that the son shall not bear the iniquity of the father, even though that iniquity be proved. In this case it was not. Whatever happens in this whole area of the relationship between the individual and the state, we will do it ourselves. It cannot be blamed on Malenkov or Mao Tse-tung or even our allies. It seems to us, that is to Fred Friendly and myself, that that should be argued endlessly.

****

ANN: It was one of the programs—this was in the fall of 1953—which, in effect, laid down the path to the McCarthy program. In 1954 he went much further.

****

The line between investigating and persecuting is a very fine one, and the Junior Senator from Wisconsin has stepped over it repeatedly. His primary achievement has been in confusing the public mind as between the internal and external effects of Communism. We must not confuse descent with disloyalty. We will not walk in fear of one another. We will not be driven by fear into an age of unreason if we dig deep into our history and our doctrine. Remember that we are not descended from fearful men. Not from men who fear to write, to speak, to associate and defend causes that were for a moment unpopular. This is no time for men who oppose Senator McCarthy's methods to remain silent or for those who approve. As a nation we've come into our full inheritance at a tender age. We program ourselves, as indeed we are, the defenders of freedom where ever it continues to exist in the world, but we cannot defend freedom abroad while deserting it at home. The actions of the Junior Senator from Wisconsin have caused alarm and dismay amongst our allies abroad and given considerable comfort to our enemies. Whose fault is that? Not really his. He didn't create this situation of fear, he exploited it, and rather successfully. Cassius was right. The fault, dear Brutus, is not in our stars, but in ourselves. Good night and good luck.

****

JASON: Ed Murrow was one of a very few people who came down on McCarthy in spite of the implications.

ANN: Right, in fact, he was the only one who did it on television. There were many courageous people who were fighting McCarthy on radio, Murrow among them, and in newspapers and magazines, but it really needed the power of television. Murrow was the only one who stood up, who actually had the authority to do so, but who also had the courage to broadcast at the height of McCarthy's power, a nationwide program calling outright for opposition to him.

JASON: And there were repercussions for him.

ANN: Quite a few. It is most likely that it ruined his career. First of all, in the 1950s, if you were in communication, it was absolute death if you stopped being a consensus figure. Today, controversy, to some small amount, gives you a little added publicity. In those days, to be labeled controversial was the worst thing that could happen to you if you were in broadcasting. What happened was— and I don't want to go into too much detail— McCarthy, in the interest of fairness, had to be offered an equivalent half hour on Murrow's program to reply. He did. He did his very best to slam Murrow any way he could. Here in the East, a lot of people were kind of smiling and saying, "Oh, he's just showing what kind of lawyer he is." In many parts of the country, in the East as well, many more people, something like two or three times the number of people watched the show, watched McCarthy, than saw Murrow in the first place. They saw McCarthy make his charges. They didn't know what he was responding to. They only knew that he was calling Murrow a Communist. Unfortunately, a good many of those people either believed him or figured maybe there's something a little wrong with this guy Murrow. Then McCarthy, in various ways, also managed to have his staff organize an underground campaign through leaks to sympathetic columnists, which got into newspapers across the country, through the people who had red baiting newsletters such as *Counterattack*. They were the same people who put out *Red Channels*, with which I know you're quite familiar. The newsletter attacked Murrow saying he was a danger, and a terrible Communist, and a traitor, etc. This newsletter went all over the country. It went to all the various media. It also went to libraries. It went to unions. It went to schools. It was picked up by sympathetic news sources. In one place, in Peoria, Illinois, they actually ran it as an editorial. The end result to Murrow's career was, in hindsight, very—very damaging, and I think it is no coincidence that that career—there were other factors at work, too—that career lasted only about four more years.

JASON: When you mention *Red Channels* and *Counterattack*, you hit a very sore nerve. I am thoroughly familiar with both yellow sheet publications and, in fact, I have a copy of *Red Channels*. Many of the guests I have had on this show have experienced devastating consequences thanks to those people and their half-cocked bits of data. It's a subject we could discuss for hours. After the McCarthy debacle, Murrow's career went another way. He began doing *Small World*, a panel discussion show and *Person to Person*.

ANN: Murrow had started *Person to Person*, which was a fluff show, in early 1953. It was simply a very soft interview program. He took a camera into people's houses and did a kind of house tour. People always wondered why he kept up with it and his reasons were varied, but it did serve a good purpose when there was a big controversy—such as McCarthy striking back at him. People would look at *Person to Person* and say, "There's nothing wrong with this guy. He's just an all-around kind of guy. Look at all those important people who are appearing on his house tour show." It did have a bit of a mitigating effect; however, it is true that Murrow's first love at the time was his documentary series, which was cancelled in 1958. That left him with *Person to Person*, about which he didn't care a whit, and a very charming sort of round table talk show called *Small World*, which, unfortunately, did not survive because, apparently, it was just not commercially viable. Murrow himself gave up *Person to Person* a year after *See It Now* was cancelled. *Person to Person* had served its purpose, and he didn't want to stay with it any longer than he absolutely had to.

JASON: I believe his final work would have been *CBS Reports*, some of the very, very dramatic documentaries including one about the migrant workers called "Harvest of Shame."

****

> *This scene is not taking place in a dark room. It has nothing to do with Johannesburg or Cape Town. It is not Nyasaland or Nigeria. This is Florida. These are citizens of the United States, 1960. This is a shape up for migrant workers. This is how the humans who harvest the food for the best fed people in the world get hired. They ride trucks. They follow the sun. They are the migrants, workers in the sweat shops of the soil, the harvest of shame.*

****

ANN: Murrow's career was in such a bad way. Beginning early in 1959 he requested a year's sabbatical, so he was away from the summer of '59 until the spring of 1960. He had always wanted to do a show about the migrant workers, but he never could quite get a handle on it. While he was away a very talented young producer, David Lowe, was asked to try to put it together. He said, "You've got it," went off and started doing things and came back with a beautiful show, one of the best of the CBS documentaries. When Murrow came back, the show was in the works. He threw himself into it. But things were going even worse after he got back from his break. You often wonder, who would have thought that this was going to be one of his last programs. There is a sadness to this piece and a beauty to it that goes even beyond what he experienced while he was taping it. By the way, being a farm boy himself, having done that kind of work, having lived in poverty, he could relate to those people.

JASON: That program remains a benchmark. Then in 1961, a guy that he had interviewed on *Person to Person*, at that time a Senator from Massachusetts, John Fitzgerald Kennedy, appointed him to head the USIA (United States Information Agency)

ACT VII: KEEPING US INFORMED

ANN: Right, Jack Kennedy had once appeared on *Person to Person* talking from his living room, and then he became President, and was in Murrow's debt. It was a matter of leaving broadcasting and literally leading American propaganda abroad although it was from Washington, DC. Murrow knew he was going to have to leave CBS. Leaving CBS meant leaving broadcasting. His reasons for making such a dramatic change were, again, many. In this case, it was most likely that the old liberal and Kennedy backer, Chester Bowles, had a lot to do with persuading him to take the job, telling him he could be a great influence. He told him he could have a lot to say about foreign policy. He said, "You can really do a lot of good for the country if you take the job." So Murrow finally decided in favor of it, which meant leaving a job that paid him about $200,000 a year for a job that paid only $25,000 a year.

JASON: Toward the end of his life he was very ill with lung cancer and finally did succumb to it in April of 1965. He left behind a monumental legacy for us all. Before he died, he spoke to the RTNDA (Radio and Television News Directors Association) about what he thought of radio news as it was then constituted, and what was happening to radio and television in general.

****

One of the basic troubles with radio and television news is that both instruments have grown up as an incompatible combination of show business, advertising, and news. Each of the three is a rather bizarre, and at times, demanding profession. And when you get all three under one roof, the dust never settles. The total management of the networks, with a few notable exceptions, has been trained in advertising, sales, research, or show business. But, by the nature of the corporate structure, they also make the final and crucial decisions having to do with news and public affairs. Frequently, they have neither the time nor the competence to do this. So far as radio, that most satisfying, ancient, but rewarding instrument is concerned, the diagnosis of the difficulties is not too difficult. In order to progress, it needs to go backward, back to the time when singing commercials were not allowed on news reports. When there was no middle commercial in a fifteen-minute news report. When radio was rather proud and alert, and fast. In this kind of complex and confusing world you cannot tell very much about the why of the news in a broadcast where only three minutes is available for the news. If radio news is to be regarded as a commodity, only acceptable when saleable, only a package to fit the advertising of a sponsor, then I don't care what you call it. I say it isn't news. This instrument can teach, it can illuminate, yes, and it can even inspire, but it can do so only to the extent that humans are determined to use it to those ends. Otherwise it's nothing but wires and lights in a box.

****

ANN: To pinpoint that in time, we have to go back to 1958. He was still in broadcasting. His program had been cancelled and while, speaking to the RTNDA in Chicago, he got up to, as he said, "Talk to the journeymen about what is happening in our industry." I think it is perhaps likely that he thought his own time was up, and there were things that he simply had to say no matter what the consequences were going to be. What he was afraid of, was a time when the public would not be getting its information, so he accused the networks, and the stations, and the entire broadcasting industry, radio and television, of decadence, escapism, and insulation from the realities of the world in which we live.

JASON: Of course, he meant commercialism.

ANN: Correct.

JASON: And, it has only gotten much worse since then.

****

Edward R. Murrow was an impossible act to follow. From his early days, right up to the end of his life, he was always a man who spoke his mind and let the chips fall where they may. He and his first hire, William L. Shirer, were called the forefathers of broadcast journalism.

We spoke earlier about his abilities as a talent scout, but we only mentioned a few of the many distinguished newsmen he assembled during World War II. We spoke of Charles Collingwood, and Richard C. Hottelet, and Winston Burdett, and Eric Sevareid, but there were many more in the group that got to be known as "Murrow's Boys." Some of the others were Howard K. Smith, Ned Calmer, Cecil Brown, Larry LeSueur, and a lady named Mary Marvin Breckinridge, all names that lasted for a long, long time. After the war he added Daniel Schorr and Robert Pierpoint. Quite a team by anyone's standards.

Mr. Murrow was honored several times with Peabody Awards, and in 1951 and 1952 he received Special George Polk Awards. Queen Elizabeth II made him an honorary Knight Commander of the Order of the British Empire. Many schools, libraries, streets and other things carry his name in memory of what he did for us all. His list of honors is much too long to be covered here, but the information is readily available from uncounted sources.

My best suggestion is to read Ann Sperber's book, *Murrow, His Life and Times*, which is still in most libraries. It is a big book, but it is well worth your time. I treasure my copy which was sent to me by the author herself. Sadly, she too passed away when she had a sudden heart attack in 1994.

ACT VIII:
NETWORK IMPRESARIO

It is nearly time to close out Volume Two, and what better way than to briefly discuss a very important element of the broadcast industry. That element is the networks, or groups of stations, working together under one general management, some of them being wholly owned with many others operating as subsidiary outlets, able to select some programs from the parent source, while rejecting others in favor of local features.

The first of these networks to take over large chunks of air time was NBC (The National Broadcasting Company), owned by Radio Corporation of America, which in turn, was owned by Westinghouse. It was an operation that was guided mostly by David Sarnoff, beginning in 1923. In 1926, NBC began operating as two separate entities, The Red Network and The Blue Network. In the early 1940s, the FCC and The Supreme Court ruled that no network would be allowed to own more than one outlet in a single city, which meant that NBC's duplicity would have to be separated from each other. In 1943, they sold off The Blue Network, which had been doing mostly news, cultural and other sustaining broadcasts, or in other words, non-sponsored material. That entity was purchased by a man named Edward Noble, the owner of Life Savers candy, and was renamed ABC (The American Broadcasting Company).

In 1928, along came William S. Paley, who desperately wanted to get into radio, and so he purchased a small eastern group called The United Network, from which he created CBS (The Columbia Broadcasting System). He is the subject of this final Act, so I will not go into any detail right here and now.

In 1934, four independent stations in New York City (WOR), Chicago (WGN), Cincinnati (WLW) and Detroit (WXYZ) banded together to form MBS (Mutual Broadcasting System), which was to become the largest group of stations ever assembled in this country.

There is so much history to be learned about each one of these conglomerates and many other smaller groups, but that is a tale for other books.

Now it is time to listen in on a conversation with a man who researched and wrote a biography, titled, *Empire, William S. Paley and the Making of CBS.*

His name is Lewis Paper. We spoke on October 15, 1987.

****

JASON: Tell me why you are qualified to tackle such a complex subject as William S Paley. I do know you've written some other very fine books in the past.

LEW: I'll let others judge how good they are. I did a book about John F. Kennedy called *The Promise & the Performance*, and a few years ago I wrote a biography of Justice Louis Brandeis.

JASON: I'll vouch for them. I've read them both.

LEW: It's always good to meet someone with fine judgment.

JASON: I don't know how to answer that except to say thanks, so let's talk about Bill Paley. He is a man who's done so much. He started out pretty much as he is today. He's always been a very dynamic person. Of course, he didn't begin his career in radio. He began in a totally unrelated business.

LEW: His father had a business manufacturing cigars, and Bill Paley was slated to take over the company, but, as he told his friends at the time, he really wanted a job where he could meet glamorous people. He decided he couldn't meet many of them in the cigar business. He fixed his sights on broadcasting. He got, through a family friend, an opportunity to purchase a controlling interest in a small, struggling radio network in New York called United Independent Broadcasters. He bought in, in 1928; two days shy of his 27th birthday. That was his start.

JASON: And within a couple of years, due to many factors, he had renamed it and was just about to be a millionaire.

LEW: He had some luck, some good business sense, and a willingness to hire and listen to people who were more experienced than he was. He was able, to the surprise of almost everyone, to make CBS a strong competitor to NBC. By the early 1930s, when most companies were going bankrupt, Bill Paley's Columbia Broadcasting System was making millions of dollars in profits.

JASON: You're talking about depression years, because '28 was when he got in, and the company was about $179,000 in debt. But in '29, which was an extremely bad year for almost everyone else, he turned a $474,000 profit.

LEW: By 1931, they were making a profit of nearly $2,000,000. That's because radio blossomed in the 1930s. People didn't have the money to go out, to have outside entertainment. Radio became like another member of the family. It brought them Franklin Roosevelt, Jack Benny, George Burns, and Will Rogers. It brought a lot of people into their homes and gave them the kind of entertainment and information they couldn't afford. With the audiences came advertisers, and with the advertisers, came big profits.

JASON: And also good talent. I'm not talking about just the actors. I'm talking about some of the real class producers, directors, and writers, some of the classic programming CBS had in those early years.

LEW: Of course, CBS did the Orson Welles *Mercury Theatre of the Air.* There was the famed episode when Orson did the invasion from Mars. People actually thought it was really happening. That was some evidence of the power of radio and how successful it really was.

JASON: Here's an interesting thought I got from Elliott Lewis, who also worked at CBS for quite some time. Elliott said that it was intriguing that "The War of the Worlds" had so many people panicking, and yet, if they switched around on the dial, and if the Martians were really attacking, how come CBS was the only network that knew about it?

LEW: I have to say that, when people turned on their radio, they didn't want to change the dial. I think that's what happened. A lot of people do that in respect to television, too.

JASON: That particular broadcast was on opposite a *Charlie McCarthy Show* where they had a guest many folks didn't want to hear. Many people switched to CBS after Orson's disclaimer.

LEW: Most of the people seemed to have switched after the disclaimer.

JASON: There were other people in those early days, a lot of fine directors. I'm thinking of Bill Robson and his joint production of *The Fall of the City*, which was a real landmark in radio history. Creatively, it was far above almost anything else I can think of.

LEW: One of the reasons they had so much quality was because, despite their huge success, Paley was not able to sell all of the time CBS had available, so there were large blocks of time that remained available to experiment with a lot of those innovative and very good programs. In fact, one of the great accidents of history was how Edward R. Murrow, who was originally hired as a director of talks to bring in school choirs, and lecturers, and symphonies, wound up becoming CBS's most famed newscaster. It was not what he was supposed to be doing at all when he was first hired.

JASON: Something happened along the way though, when he was over in England with a war getting started. Murrow just simply fell into it.

LEW: He happened to have been there. He and Bill Shirer were in Europe when Hitler moved into Austria. Murrow moved on to Austria and Shirer went back to London. The two of them, because CBS thought of them as eyewitnesses, thought they would have to rely on their on-scene accounts. It became the first opportunity for Murrow to demonstrate his talents as a newscaster.

JASON: Bill Paley pulled off some pretty terrific deals through the years. He was a salesman more than anything else. He could sell ideas to you whether you thought you needed them or not. I'm thinking about a deal he worked with Adolph Zukor and Paramount, when he desperately needed some cash flow early on.

LEW: That was really an interesting combination. Zukor was the head of Paramount Pictures. Interestingly enough, Zukor and other movie moguls were interested in broadcasting because they thought, at the time, that television was right around the corner. They wanted to have an interest in broadcasting, so that they would not have to worry about the competition. Zukor came in and gave Paley an offer, and Paley was able to work out a deal so that he could have the money, and ultimately, keep the stock that he had bought from Zukor. When it came time to buy back the Paramount stock, Zukor didn't have the money, so he couldn't complete the deal. It was a complicated arrangement, but it did show that Bill Paley, even at that young age, was charming, confident, and shrewd.

JASON: The depression fell right into the middle of that, because the stock was worth about $65 a share in twenty-eight. When the time came for Paramount to buy them back at $85, as the original deal had been made, their stock was only worth nine bucks.

LEW: Right, so it turned out to be a great deal. Nobody anticipated the depression any more than people anticipated the recent drop in the markets.

JASON: Let's go back a little further. In talking about Bill Paley and his ability to handle people, he was only a teenager when his father went to his grandfather's funeral in Chicago. He had to take care of a whole big labor situation in Philadelphia.

LEW: He spent a lot of time working with his father, so he had a good sense of what his father wanted—how his father ran the business. His father was an incredibly successful businessman himself. Sam Paley saw that his son Bill had a great maturity and was capable of minding the store, so to speak. Paley, even then, had developed the ability to talk to people and persuade them. He was successful in fighting back. It all centered on his company's willingness to reach a deal with some striking laborers. He had to work out a deal with the laborers and fend off the competing cigar manufacturers, who were angry with him for working with the strikers.

JASON: One thing Bill Paley always did, or tried to do, was to pay people what they were worth rather than what he could get them for.

LEW: That's very true, and that applied to programming as well. That was the big difference between him and David Sarnoff at NBC. Once he decided that somebody was a hit, whether it was Will Rogers, or Amos 'n' Andy, or Jack Benny, he would pay whatever it took to get that person to his network. Sarnoff, in contrast, had a very dim view of performers and thought that they were beneath him. As a result, he was not really competing with Paley because he was not prepared to spend the kind of money that Paley was prepared to spend.

JASON: They had completely different childhoods. I wonder if that had anything to do with it.

LEW: I think so. I think all of us are a reflection of our environment to a large extent. You had Bill Paley who grew up very wealthy. His father took vicarious pleasure in watching his son indulge himself and did, in fact, urge his son to indulge himself and spend money. He often had the benefit of watching his father in business and seeing how his father catered to public tastes in cigar manufacturing, how he marketed them. That was a tremendous advantage. Sarnoff, in contrast, came from Russia at the age of twelve and could barely speak a word of English. He did not have the kind of formal education that Paley did, did not have the same kind of father and tutelage. I think those differences showed up, not only in the way they approached their business, but also in their lifestyle.

JASON: In talking about bidding wars between Paley and Sarnoff, one of the early battles was over Bing Crosby, who wanted much more than Sarnoff was willing to give him.

LEW: That's right. Paley heard Crosby on a record while he was on a ship sailing to Europe. He immediately wired back to his people at CBS, "Hire singer named Crosby!" There were a lot of questions back in New York as to whether they should do that, because they had checked it out and found out that Crosby frequently liked to drink and was often unreliable. He couldn't show up for performances. They decided not to do it because of that unreliability. When Paley came back and found out they hadn't hired him, and found out that NBC was chasing after Crosby, he got really angry and said to his staff, "I didn't ask you to check out whether it was a good deal or not. I told you to hire him!" I remember, I talked to one of the secretaries who worked at the place at that time. This was in 1931. She remembered that when they finally did sign Crosby, Terry Talley brought him around to the office and introduced him to everybody. There were only about twenty people working there at the time. He introduced Crosby to everyone as the new star of the network. It would be a lot more difficult today for Paley to go around and introduce a new performer to all the employees they have now.

JASON: Crosby was a pretty new performer. He had been singing with Paul Whiteman, but he certainly didn't have a big name in those days.

LEW: No, he didn't. That came with Paley and working for CBS.

JASON: There were quite a few people that he hired who stayed with him for many years and did the work that they had to do, even though they were completely different personalities. First off, I'm thinking of Ed Klauber.

LEW: Klauber was a complete contrast of personality. He had come from the *New York Times*, and people there didn't like him at all. While he was a good journalist, a lot of people thought he was mean spirited, not at all a good administrator, at least, *vis-a-vis* people. He was then hired by Paley's public relations council, a guy named Bernays. Ed Bernays was the one who hired Klauber and brought him over to the news department. Nobody liked him there, either. Paley needed an administrator. Paley was not a good administrator. He often didn't like to pay attention to detail. Bernays recommended that Paley hire Klauber and Paley met with him. Klauber was in his early forties and Paley was about thirty. He seemed like an old man. Klauber was gruff, kind of a taciturn guy, not at all the kind of charming *bon-vivant* that Paley was. Paley called Bernays back and said, "This guy Klauber doesn't seem at all right to me." Bernays, who was persistent, said "Give him another chance. He has the kind of talents you need." So, Paley was persuaded and when he hired Klauber, one of the first things Klauber did was to fire Bernays, saying that they didn't have to spend the money to have a public relations council. Paley came to rely on Klauber a tremendous amount. Klauber was very responsible for shaping a lot of the news policies under which Murrow and Shirer and all those other people flourished. People had a great respect for him.

JASON: He's the one who wanted to keep the news completely neutral rather than have commentary, because they got burned a few times in those early days.

LEW: I think that Klauber used to say to Paley, "Look, a news organization has a tremendous responsibility to the public, because the public can only discriminate, tell the difference, between things they know. I presume they can tell the difference between a good can of peaches and a bad can of peaches. All they have to do is taste them, but the public can't tell the difference, so often, between a good radio station and a bad one. They just believe what they hear. So, because there's that dependence, it imposes an even greater obligation on us to be fair and to give the public both sides of opinions, both sides of any controversial issue. We must make sure the public has access to the information and that the news isn't slanted." Paley was very persuaded by that. Most of the time, Klauber's judgments were good, although some of his ideas were not so good. One idea that Klauber had, and that Paley bought in the early 1940s, was a proposal that congress enact a law to have the Federal Communications Commission license networks, which would only increase the government's control over the networks. That was one of the few occasions when Klauber misfired.

JASON: Wasn't Paley's concept of equal time one of the first? You know, when someone stated an opinion, the opposing side should have a chance to rebut it.

Wasn't he one of the originators of that idea?

LEW: I wouldn't call him the originator. The notion of providing equal opportunity and balance was really something that had been first suggested by the Federal Radio Commission. It became part of the new FCC law in 1934, but Paley was certainly one of those forcefully advocating that and interpreting it in both letter and spirit. His support was instrumental in giving the concept legitimacy.

JASON: And putting it to use.

LEW: Right, like in 1936 when Earl Browder was the Communist candidate for president. Time had been given to Roosevelt and Alf Landon, so Browder came by to say that he wanted time, too. After all, he was a legitimate candidate. Everybody in the press and elsewhere said that Browder should not get on because he was a Communist. Paley said, "I'm not going to sit here and judge his opinions. He is a candidate, and the law requires me to be fair, to give all candidates an equal opportunity, and I'm going to do that." He got a lot of hate mail because of that. He felt very committed to that principal of fairness.

JASON: He ran into some problems even before that. I'm talking about Father Coughlin and also about George Bernard Shaw at one time. They never had any idea what these guys might say once they got on the air.

LEW: It was all live in those days. George Bernard Shaw came on one night and said, "Hello America, you old boobs," or something like that. He kept using the air to praise Russia, which was very embarrassing for CBS. Those kinds of things don't happen anymore because very few things are live, or when they are, they have a delay and a dump button available.

JASON: A lot of hilarious things happened on live radio, but many of them weren't so funny.

LEW: Absolutely right.

JASON: Let's talk a bit about Paul Kesten. He came out of the ad world. He was about the same age as Paley.

LEW: They got along okay. Kesten was the exact opposite of Klauber, handsome guy, very smooth, very polished. He had such a concern about his appearance that he used to polish the bottoms of his shoes. In case he put his feet up on the desk, he wanted to look good. He and Paley got along really well. They were contemporaries, had similar personalities, similar outlooks. He was somebody who really helped to establish CBS's image for quality and helped market them very successfully. This was in the 1930s.

JASON: And in the middle of the '30s along came Frank Stanton. He was there for a long time. He was the president of the corporation for twenty-three years.

LEW: Stanton was there from 1935 until he retired in 1973. He came in thirty-five, as a research assistant, and he climbed all the way to the top, right underneath Paley.

JASON: He and Paul Lazarsfeld were the two people who began the concept of market research for radio.

LEW: That's true. They developed a system they called "Little Annie." It was relatively simple. It seems to defy all current notions about how to access the public's reactions to programs. They would pull in people off the street in New York, or Los Angeles, or Chicago and have them sit in a studio, and watch a program, and press little buttons to record their reactions to something funny, or sad, good, or not good. They were people selected at random. A lot of experts scoffed at the idea saying it wasn't scientific enough. It proved to be very effective in enabling CBS to predict which programs would be successful and which would not. It was a system that was widely used by them for many years.

JASON: Aside from being wrapped up in obtaining new affiliates, and selling, and so on, Paley's main function, and what he liked best, was programming.

LEW: He just did not want to mess with the details of administration. He left that to Klauber, and after Klauber, Stanton. He very rarely got involved with administration. He focused his energy on programming and having a good time for himself. He would go out to California frequently. He would have dinner with the stars, people like Jack Benny or George Burns, to keep them happy. He'd try to develop new program ideas. That's what he focused on. That's why he was in broadcasting in the first place. He wanted to be where the glamour was, so that's what he did.

JASON: He had a good eye for programs. He knew pretty well what would sell, but he made some interesting mistakes a couple of times. I'm talking about one in particular in the early days of television involving Lucille Ball and Desi Arnaz. He felt their program had no future. He didn't want it at first.

LEW: Harry Ackerman, his programming executive in

California, was the guy who had to persuade him. Lucille was having marital problems with Desi Arnaz. They came with this radio program she had done called *My Favorite Husband*. They wanted to transport it over to television. She said she wouldn't do it unless Desi could be her husband. Everybody was against that. They said, "What kind of a role can a struggling Cuban band leader play in a show about an American couple?" Originally, they said there was no way. Paley said it was ridiculous that Desi could have a part. But Lucille, who was very talented and very much in demand said, "If you want me you're going to have to take Desi." She didn't want him traveling around without her. Paley finally yielded and they worked out the concept that was, ultimately, adopted of her being married to this struggling band leader and the rest, as they say, is history.

JASON: I'm not trying to nit-pick. I remember a comment that a guy named Cecil B. DeMille made about Carole Lombard, about how she'd never make it. They all make mistakes no matter how good they are. Another obvious one was *All in the Family*.

LEW: Paley was very much opposed to *All in the Family* because he saw the program and thought it was too vulgar. He thought Archie Bunker was too coarse to be part of the CBS network. He didn't like to see people speaking epithets and speaking the crass way that Archie did, but his programming executive said, "Listen, the audiences we're getting are too old. We have to expand, reach out to younger people. We have to do shows that are relevant to what is going on in the country, with all the social controversy." One of the people who were primarily pushing it was a guy named Robert Wood, who was a very conservative Republican, but thought it was the way to go. Paley was the kind of guy who was willing to delegate authority to those who wanted to take it. He was willing to do it as long as they performed. So, he gave *All in the Family* a chance. He let himself be pushed into it. Of course, the results were spectacular.

JASON: To be perfectly honest, the first time I saw that show I said, "They've got to be kidding!" I couldn't quite believe it, and I'm no prude.

LEW: Most people said that. I'm sure Paley winced a lot during that first broadcast. The public loved it.

JASON: There is no question where it went from there. It would be impossible to go in depth into a book as laden with information as your volume, *Empire: William S. Paley and the Making of CBS*, in the time we have. Let's jump forward a bunch of years. As recently as 1986, at the age of eighty-four, Bill Paley came back to take charge of CBS, along with Laurence Tisch. What's going on over there? You have better contacts than I, or any of my people, do.

LEW: What happened was, Paley kept saying he wanted to retire, but he really didn't. Every time he found a so-called successor, he found some reason to fire him. It was creating a lot of instability. Finally, the Board came to him in 1982, when he was in his early 80s and literally forced him to retire. They brought in Tom Wyman. Wyman became Chairman and Chief Operating Officer. Paley was not content to be retired. He wanted to be where the action was. As he told David Sarnoff, "They're going to have to carry me out with my boots on." He waited until Wyman faltered. Then CBS suffered some financial setbacks and Ted Turner tried to chase after them.

There were some bad acquisitions, some bad business deals, and Paley started to talk to people about the fact that Wyman, at least in his view, was ruining the company. One person who shared that view was Larry Tisch, who had bought a lot of CBS stock and was very interested himself in getting more actively involved in broadcasting. Tisch decided that he could run things better than Tom Wyman. Between Tisch and Paley, they owned one third of the company. So Tisch went to Paley and said, "I think we should get rid of Wyman. We can bring you back into the company." When they brought Paley back, he became the vehicle in which Tisch, too, could come in and do something that he very much wanted to do, which was run a broadcast network. So, although Paley came back and was Chairman of the Board, he was then eighty-six with some limitations to his energy. Now, the one really calling the shots there is Larry Tisch. The bottom line of it all is that Paley's back where he always wanted to be. He's got his office on the thirty-fifth floor of Black Rock, CBS headquarters. I think he'll stay there as long as he wants.

JASON: They probably will carry him out with his boots on some day.

LEW: They probably will.

****

Not long after this discussion, William S. Paley passed away due to kidney failure. There is no doubt that what he built was a monumental accomplishment. I'll go into more detail on the subject in the Afterword.

Afterword/Finale
Murrow, Paley and the CBS Tie-Ins

Good friends they were. I am referring once more to Ed Murrow and Bill Paley. Their friendship was much more than your usual employer-employee relationship. When Mr. Paley married Barbara 'Babe' Cushing in 1947, Mr. Murrow was the only CBS person invited to the wedding. It was something that rankled some of Ed's co-workers but, the long-standing Paley-Murrow connection had developed during the war years and would never be broken. That is not to say that there were not some problems along the way but, there was only one that created a serious temporary rift between them.

It all came about during the summer of 1950 when Ed Murrow traveled to Korea to report on the events taking place there. After a careful scrutiny of what was transpiring there; Ed Murrow found it necessary to express how he felt about the situation, particularly about a recent battle that was waged in the southern part of Korea, where there was nothing to accomplish, except to be able to claim a victory in an area where things had been going well. He said it was a foolish waste of assets, and he added:

****

When we start moving up through dead valleys, to villages to which we have put the torch by retreating—What then of the people who live there? They have lived on the knife edge of despair and disaster for centuries. Their pitiful possessions have been consumed by the flames of war. Will our re-occupation of that flea-bitten land lessen or increase the attraction of Communism?

****

His comments were never aired, which made Murrow furious. It seemed that almost everyone in the news department, and even Bill Paley, felt that he had overstepped his authority and broken the rules. Ed Chester, the director of news, said that if they ran it there might be legal problems.

To this Murrow responded:

****

In Asia, there is no greater crime than to destroy a man's rice bowl. It would only draw the masses to Communism.

****

The dispute was never truly settled, and no one was happy.

One of the things that Bill Paley was concerned about was that the Korean report would draw further criticism from Senator Joe McCarthy and his gang of rabble-rousers. It was not until several years later that Ed Murrow and his co-producer Fred Friendly took the hideous McCarthy on full bore on *See it Now*. At that time, in respect for their friendship, Bill Paley refused to preview the program before air time. He thought he owed that much to Mr. Murrow. He also suggested that they offer the Junior Senator from Wisconsin equal time to respond before McCarthy demanded it, thereby, beating him to the punch. As was previously stated in the interview with Ann Sperber, many more people saw the response than had seen the original program that caused it. The end result was that Joe McCarthy's popularity dropped off the map in spite of his effort to publicize his own point of view. When he attempted to defuse Murrow's statements, he created the final straw in his own demise. It was only a few months later, in December of that same year, that Joe McCarthy was censured by his colleagues in the Senate for his over-aggressive tactics. The vote was 67 to 22 against him. In reality, one of the most visible reasons for his downfall was the Murrow-Paley-Friendly team at CBS.

When speaking of Edward R. Murrow, it is important to bring up his long-term connection with the aforementioned Fred Friendly. It was partly due to Mr. Murrow's strong suggestion that CBS hired

Fred away from NBC in order to produce for him. They made an interesting and dynamic team. Fred and Ed were two diametrically opposed personalities. Fred was all of the things that Ed was not and *vice-versa*. He was a large man, four inches over six feet tall. He was volatile and flamboyant while Ed was a mostly calm person. They complemented each other and worked very well together. The first series they did was called *Hear it Now*, and before long, it went on television as *See it Now*, a program that had great success for several years. They were willing and able to take on many of the most difficult problems of that time.

Another man who must be mentioned from the Paley-Murrow team at CBS is Ed Klauber. As we found out while discussing him with Lew Paper, he was not an easy man to get along with. That was not at all the case with Ed Murrow's association with him. They worked very well together, more often than not. In fact, Ed Klauber was the man who asked Murrow to become the European director of CBS way back in 1937.

In 1960, Ed Murrow did a tribute to Ed Klauber calling him a great editor who was dedicated to the pursuit of truth.

Much more could be said about the inner workings of the CBS news team and the network in general but, I will leave it up to you to read the two books I recommended earlier about Mr. Murrow and Mr. Paley and some of their many cohorts. Both books are easy to find.

BIBLIOGRAPHY

Barnouw, Erik. *The Golden Web: A History of Broadcasting in the United States: Volume II 1933 to 1953*, Oxford University Press, USA (1968)

Briggs, Lord Asa. *The BBC: The First Fifty Years*, Oxford University Press, USA (1985)

Dunning, John. *On the Air: The Encyclopedia of Old-Time Radio*, Oxford University Press, USA (1998)

Milligan, Spike. *The Goon Show Scripts*, First Sphere Books Edition, London (1973)

Morgan, Henry. *Here's Morgan! The Original BAD BOY of Broadcasting*, Barricade Books, New York (1994)

Nachman, Gerald. *Raised on Radio*, University of California Press, Berkeley & Los Angeles (1998)

Paper, Lewis J. *Empire: William S. Paley and the Making of CBS*, St. Martin's Press, New York (1987)

Sperber, A. M. *Murrow: His Life and Times*, Freundlich Books, New York (1986) (1987)

INDEX

2

26 by Corwin, 265
2BD, 6
2BE, 6
2DE, 6
2EH, 6
2LO, 6
2LS, 6
2MT, 6
2WP, 6
2ZY, 6

5

5IT, 6
5NG, 6
5NO, 6
5PY, 6
5SC, 6
5SX, 6
5WR, 6

6

64 Cent Question, The (Bob and Ray), 216
6BM, 11
6FL, 11
6KH, 11
6LV, 11
6ST, 11

7

77 Sunset Strip, 72

A

Abbott Mysteries, 82
Ackerman, Harry S., 315
Addams Family, The, 99, 273-4
Adventures of Kit Carson, The, 255
Adventures of Sam Spade, 240
AFRA (American Federation of Radio Artists), 54, 72
AFTRA (American Federation of Television and Radio Artists), 72, 80
Alan Young Show, 34
Albertson, Jack, 42
Alfred Hitchcock Presents, 83
All in the Family, 316, 317
Allen, Fred, 33, 34, 187-9, 209
Allen, Steve, 270
Allen, Woody, 99, 248
Allison, Fran, 123-136
Ameche, Don, 57, 77, 94, 217
Ameche, James 'Jim', 217
Ames, Leon, 42, 47
Ames, Nancy (TW3 Girl), 194
Amos 'n' Andy, 75, 96, 97, 308
Amsterdam, Morey, 123

André, Pierre, 91
Andy Griffith Show, The, 274
Antis, Jerry, 34
Apache, 255
Aristocats, The, 206
Armed Forces Radio Service, 70, 195
Arnaz, Desi, 43, 315, 316
Arquette, Cliff, 114
Arthur Godfrey Time, 124
Ashenhurst, Ann, 75
Aunt Jenny's Real Life Stories, 198
Aunt Mary, 259
Autry, Gene, 229

B

Bachelor's Children, 90, 91, 92, 93
Backus, Jim, 31, 202
Bad Day at Black Rock, 229
Baer, Parley, 60, 95, 238, 240, 244, 257-275
Baileys of Balboa, The, 252
Ball, Lucille 'Lucy', 45, 315, 316
Bambi, 233
Barnes, Paul, 58
Barrymore, Lionel, 263
Bartell, Harry, 238, 260, 270
Baruch, Andre, 29
Batman, 99
Beck, Jackson, 78, 221
Beemer, Brace, 65
Begley, Ed, 32, 44
Benaderet, Bea, 69, 268, 269, 270
Benchley, Robert, 196
Bennett, Constance, 182
Benny, Jack, 35, 66, 188-9, 196, 199, 305, 315
Bentine, Michael, 14, 20
Berle, Milton, 203
Bernard, Tommy, 70

Bernays, Edward L. 'Ed', 311
Berry, Bob, 180, 214
Betty and Bob, 76, 77
Biden, Joseph, 215
Big Story, 82
Blanc, Mel, 34, 48, 271
Boardman Jr., True, 251
Bonanza, 88, 99, 229
Boone, Richard 'Dick', 234
Borglum, Lincoln, 82
Bowles, Chester, 299
Bradbury, Ray, 246
Brando, Marlon, 207
Brave New World, 263-5
Breakfast Club, The, 106, 124-7
Breckinridge, Mary Marvin, 301
Brice, Fanny, 196
Bridal Crown, The, 232
Bridges, Jeffrey, 'Jeff', 255
Briggs, Asa, 7
British Broadcasting Company, Ltd., 6
British Broadcasting Corporation, 7
British Thompson-Houston Company, 6
Browder, Earl R., 313
Brown, Himan, 87
Brown, Cecil, 301
Brown, Himan 'Hi', 80, 82
Brownstone Theatre, 78
Bryan, Arthur Q., 69, 114
Bulldog Drummond, 182
Burdett, Winston, 283, 284, 301
Burke, Billie, 45
Burns and Allen Show, 40, 45
Burns, George, 36, 40, 305, 315
Burr, Raymond, 229, 244
Buster Brown, 233, 236-7

INDEX

C

Cagney, James, 85
Calmer, Ned, 301
Camden Theatre, 16
Cantor, Eddie, 30, 31, 33, 198
Captain Midnight, 58, 92
Captain Midnight TV Show, 93
Captain Stubby and the Buccaneers, 125
Captain Video and His Video Rangers, 201
Carey, Macdonald, 78, 95
Carney, Art, 32, 184
Cash McCall, 275
Cavalcade of America, 199
CBS Mystery Theatre, 266
CBS Radio Workshop, 245, 263, 265
CBS Reports, 297
Chandu, the Magician, 76
Chappell, Ernest E. 'Ernie', 82
Chase, Ilka, 182
Chekhov, Michael, 232
Chester, Ed, 320
Chesterfield Supper Club, The, 76
Chicago Theatre of the Air, 59, 79, 95
Chicago Tribune, 75, 96
Chico and the Man, 42
Child's History of the World, A, 196
Children's Corner, 182
Children's Hour, The Horn and Hardart, 69, 197
Chipmunks, The, 47
Christy, Ken, 44
Cisco Kid, The, 270
Claire (Weber), Marian, 59, 80
Clara, Lu and Em, 120-30
Close, Glenn, 255

Club Matinee, 128, 129
Coleman, Ron, 62
Collingwood, Charles, 283, 284, 288, 301
Command Performance, 195
Como, Perry, 76
Conrad, William 'Bill', 238, 240, 244, 247, 260, 270, 272
Conried, Hans, 262
Cooper, Gary, 229
Corwin, Norman, 196, 246, 265
Coughlin, Charles E. (Father Coughlin), 313
Count of Monte Cristo, The, 240, 270
Counterattack, 296
Couple Next Door, The, 98
Courage, the Cowardly Dog, 206
Cowling, Sam, 125
Creator, 249-50, 255
Crenna, Richard 'Dick', 69
Crest Fallen Manor, 129
Croft, Mary Jane, 270
Crosby, Bing, 76, 85, 310
Crosby, Bob, 79
Crowder, Connie, 60
Curley, Leo, 59
Cushing, Barbara 'Babe', 319

D

Dallas, 317
Deacon, Richard, 42
Death Valley Days, 199
Defense Attorney, 259
Dehner, John, 231-55, 257, 260, 265, 266, 270
del Valle, Jaime, 270
Delmar, Kenny, 33, 34
DeMille, Cecil B., 126, 316

"Descent of the Gods", 196
Desmond, Johnny, 126
Devine, Jerry, 259
Dick Van Dyke Show, The, 72
Dinehart, Jr., Alan, 44
Disney, Walt, 206, 232-3
Dixon, Pat, 12
Dobkin, Larry, 238, 240, 245, 260, 270
Doris Day Show, The, 252
Dorsey, Tommy, 207
Dr. Christian, 198
Dr. Ok (Bob and Ray), 216
Dragnet, 99
"Dreaded Batter Pudding Hurler, The," 20-28
Duck Tales, 47
Duff, Howard, 84
Dunlap, Patricia 'Pat', 93
Dunne, Irene, 85
Durante, Jimmy, 33
Dynasty, 217

E

Eastwood, Clint, 229
Easy Aces, 198-9
Eckersley, Peter, 7
Edwards, Jack, 262
Edwards, Sam, 262
Elders, Harry, 80
Ellery Queen, 82
Ellington, Ray, 13
Elliott, Bob (Bob and Ray), 211-28
Elliotte, John, 66
Ellis, Anthony 'Tony', 242
Ellis, Georgia, 238
Erickson, Louise, 268
Escape, 233, 234, 240, 243-4, 271

F

F Troop, 12
Falcon Crest, 217
Fall of the City, The, 307
Family Skeleton, 233, 259
Fangs (Holy Wednesday), 84
Fantasia, 233
Fastest Gun Alive, 255
Fennelly, Parker, 33, 80
Fenneman, George, 29
Fibber McGee and Company, 118
Fibber GcGee and Molly, 65, 105-121, 125
Fields, Gracie, 31
Fields, W. C., 70
Fifth Row Center, 53
Finch, Dee, 215
First Nighter, 53, 55, 58, 77, 78, 80, 92, 94, 95, 96, 99, 268
Flash Gordon, 74
Flynn, Bess, 93
Flynn, Charles, 93
Flynn, Errol, 260
Foote, Bruce, 59
Ford, Glenn, 255
Ford, Paul, 252
Fort Laramie, 229
Fortune Cookie, 84
Francis Goes to West Point, 85
Frawley, William, 44
Freleng, Isadore 'Friz', 206
Friendly Wachenheimer, Ferdinand 'Fred', 294, 320
From Here to Eternity, 207-8
Frontier Gentleman, 239, 242
Frost, David, 194

G

Gallant Hours, The, 85

Garfield, John, 206
Garish Summit (Bob and Ray), 217
Garner, James 'Jim', 255, 275
Garner, Peggy Ann, 207
Garroway, Dave, 196
Geldray, Max, 9-20
General Electric Company, 6
Gerson, Betty Lou, 53, 60
GI Jive, 195
Gingay, Ferdinand, 270
Gleason, Jackie, 184
Godfrey, Arthur, 124, 186
Goldbergs, The, 198-9, 203
Goon Show, 9, 12, 13, 14, 15, 17, 18, 19, 20-8, 36, 223
Gordon, Dorothy Lerner, 182
Gordon, Gale, 62, 63, 75, 112-14, 268
Goulding, Ray, 211-28
Granada TV, 35, 36, 38
Granby's Green Acres, 268, 269
Grand Central Station, 76
Grand Hotel, 53, 77, 80, 94
Grandstand Thrills, 97, 98
Granger, Stewart, 250
Grapevine Rancho, 129
Grappelli, Stephan, 11
Gray Ghost, The, 83
Great Gildersleeve, The, 65-71, 107, 11
Green Acres (Television), 269
Green, Bernie, 187
Green Hornet, The, 49
Greenslade, Wallace, 17, 18
Gregg, Virginia, 238, 245, 260
Guiding Light, The, 53
Gunsmoke, 95, 99, 229, 231, 238, 240-243, 257, 267, 271-3

H

"Hail and Farewell" (CBS Workshop), 246
Haller, Jan, 34
Hallmark Hall of Fame, 77
Hallmark Playhouse, 263, 266
Halls of Ivy, The, 62-4
Hanley, Tom, 243
Halop, Florence, 183
Hanna-Barbara, 206
Hannon, Marge, 93
Hansel and Gretel, 132
Harris, Phil, 66
Hart, John Lewis 'Johnny' (B.C. Comic), 222
Hartzell, Clarence, 60
"Harvest of Shame", 297-8
Hausner, Jerry, 245, 252
Have Gun – Will Travel, 229, 231, 234-35, 238, 241, 242, 248
Hay, Bill, 96, 97
Hayworth, Rita, 33
Hear it Now, 291, 321
Heavenly Days!, 121
Henry Morgan Show, The, 183, 203
Hercules in New York, 209
Here We Go Again, 121
Here's Morgan, 180
Heremans, Jean, 250
High Noon, 229
Hilton, James, 263
Hilversum One, 10
Hines, Connie, 47
Hitler, Adolph, 280, 283, 307
Hoffman, Dustin, 247-8
Holy Wednesday (Fangs), 84
Home Surgery Kit, The (Bob and Ray), 221

Homer & Jethro, 126
Honest Harold, the Homemaker, 270
Hope, Bob, 207
Horton, Edward Everett, 76
Hot Club de France, The, 11
Hottelet, Richard C., 283, 301
Houseman, John, 29, 89, 200, 254
Hudson, Rock, 247
Hume, Benita, 62
Hummert, Ann, 76
Hummert, Frank, 76
Hunter, 83
Hurt, Marlin, 114
Huxley, Aldous, 263

I

I Love a Mystery, 76
I Love Lucy Show, 44
I've Got a Secret, 193, 202
Idleson, Bill, 60
Inner Sanctum Mysteries, 76
Irving, Charles, 127
Irwin, John, 271
It Grows on Trees, 85
It's a Mad, Mad, Mad, Mad World, 209
ITV, 7, 36

J

Jack and Maude Brooks Tent Show, 87, 88
Jack Armstrong, the All American Boy, 76, 77, 90, 217
Jack Benny Show, The, 202
Jack Headstrong, the All American American (Bob and Ray), 217
Jackie Gleason – Les Tremayne Show, The, 79
Jagged Edge, 255
James, Bill, 243

Jellison, Bob 'Bobby', 58
Johnson, Raymond Edward, 55
Jolson, Al, 33, 198
Jones, Spike, 187
Jordan, Jim, 103-21, 125
Jordan, Marian, 103-118, 121 125
Judge, The, 239, 242

K

Kalb, Marvin L., 281
Kaltenmeyer's Kindergarten, 105
Kaplan, Marvin, 1209
Kate Smith Show, The, 76
Kazan, Elia, 207
KCET, 265
KDKA, 105
Kearns, Joseph 'Joe', 44
Keating. Larry, 39, 42
Kelly, Grace, 229
Kemper, Ray, 243
Kendall, Cy, 199
Kennedy, John Fitzgerald, 298
Kerns, Joe, 270
Kesten, Paul, 314
KFAC, 233
KFWB, 253
Kilgallen, Dorothy, 182
King, Larry, 269
Kirby, Durward, 127
Kirkland, Jack, 207
Kirkwood, Jack, 43
Klauber, Ed, 311, 312, 314, 315, 321
Kraft Music Hall, 76
KSL, 259, 267
Kukla, Fran and Ollie, 130, 194
Kuklapolitans, 134
Kuralt, Charles, 281

L

Ladd, Alan, 229, 233
Lancaster, Burt, 255
Landon, Alfred M. 'Alf', 313
Lane, Allan 'Rocky', 41
Lang, Harry, 271
Larson, Eric, 233
Laugh and Swing Club, The, 183
Laughton, Charles, 33
Lazarsfeld, Paul F., 314
Leave it to the Girls, 182
Lee, Peggy, 207
Left Handed Gun, The, 249, 253-4, 255
LeGrand, Richard 'Dick', 69
Lemmon, Jack, 84
LeSueur, Larry, 301
Let's Pretend, 197-8
Lewis, Elliott, 244, 245, 266, 306
Liberace, 34
Liberty Magazine, 42
Life Can Be Beautiful, 76
Life with Luigi, 76
Little Jim Dandy Burglary Kit, The (Bob and Ray), 221
Little Lulu, 206
Little Orphan Annie, 90, 92
Little, Cleavon, 251-2
Lombard, Carole, 316
Lone Journey, 182
Lone Ranger, The, 49, 65, 92
Lonely Women, 53, 54
Lon, Alice, 126
Look Who's Laughing, 121
Lord & Thomas Ad Agency, 96
Loughrane, Basil, 97
Lowe, David, 298
Lubin, Arthur, 40, 41, 42, 47

Lucy Show, The, 274
Luddy, Barbara, 55, 56, 77, 94, 263
Luke and Mirandy, 106
Lum and Abner, 268
Lux Radio Theatre, 83, 266
Lynde, Paul, 252

M

Ma Perkins, 49, 53, 54, 76
Macdonnell, Norman, 234, 237-8, 242, 245, 271
MacGraw, Ali, 254
Mad Magazine, 196
Mahoney, Con, 20
Mahoney, Jean, 34
Mahoney, Tom, 34
Man with the Golden Arm, The, 206-8
March of Time, 98
March, Hal, 32, 37
Marconi Company, 6
Markle, Fletcher, 259, 266
Mary Backstayge, Noble Wife, (Bob and Ray), 215
Mather, Jack, 271
Maverick, 229, 255
McCambridge, Mercedes, 53, 233, 259
McCarthy, Joseph R., 278, 292, 294-6, 297, 320
McConnell, Ed, 236
McCormick, Colonel Robert R., 79-80, 95-6
McNeill, Don, 124-7, 135
Meet Mr. Morgan, 180
Melba, Dame Nellie, 6
Melton, James, 59
Melton, Sid, 95
Mercury Theatre of the Air, The, 200

Meston, John, 273
Metropolitan-Vickers Company, 6
Miller, Marvin, 55, 60, 78
Milligan, Spike, 9, 14, 16, 17, 20
Miner, Jan, 78
Mister Jaw, 206
Mitchell, John N. (Attorney General), 277
Mitchum, Robert "Bob", 254
Monitor, 214
Moore, Gary, 129
Monty Python, 9
Morgan, Claudia, 80, 81
Morgan, Henry, 179-97, 201, 221
Morgan, Jane, 270
Morrison, Bret, 58, 60, 78
Morse, Carlton E., 77, 216, 233,
Mowbray, Alan, 44
Mr. Ed, 35, 36, 39, 40, 41, 42, 47, 52
Mr. Trace (Bob and Ray), 216-7
Munsters, The, 99
Muppet Show, The, 16
Murrow, Edward R., 275-302, 306, 318-321
Mussolini, Benito, 280
My Favorite Husband, 316
My World and Welcome to It, 192

N

Naish, J. Carrol, 76
National Student Federation of America (NSFA), 281
NBC University Theatre of the Air, 263
Nelson, David, 70
Nelson, Frank, 262, 271
Nelson, Ozzie, 106, 262
Newman, Paul, 249

Night Court, 74
Night of Grand Opera, A, 7
No Time for Sergeants, 207
Noel, Dick, 126
Nolan, Jeanette, 260, 265
Nordine, Ken, 127-8
North by Northwest, 84
Novarro, Ramon, 250
NRA (National Recovery Agency, The), 89

O

O'Connor, Donald, 42, 85
O'Henry Twins, The, 104
O'Toole, Peter, 250, 255
Oboler, Arch, 190, 266
Old Gold Show, The, 79
Oliver, Edna May, 199
Olsen and Johnson Show, 105
One Fells'a Family (Bob and Ray), 216
One Man's Family, 49, 76, 82, 216
Ozzie and Harriet Show, The, 70

P

Pacific Pioneer Broadcasters, 55, 58, 81, 97
Packard, Stan, 35
Page, Gale, 126
Page, Gloria, 270
Page, Patti, 126
Pal, George, 84
Palance, Jack, 229
Paley, Samuel, 308
Paley, William S., 303-321
Paper, Lewis J., 303-318
Passage to India, A, 263
Passer, Ivan, 250
Paul, Norm, 35
Payne, Virginia, 53, 82

PBS Children's Film Festival, 135
Peabodys, The, 130
Peary, Harold 'Hal', 58, 59, 65, 66, 67, 107, 111, 270
Peerce, Jan, 59
Perrin, Vic, 238, 260, 270
Perry Mason, 83
Person to Person, 297
Petticoat Junction, 269
Phil Harris-Alice Faye Show, The, 69
Phillip Marlowe, 240, 271
Phillip Morris Show, 200
Phillips, Erna, 53
Piels Brothers – Bert and Harry (Bob and Ray), 222
Pierpont, Robert, 301
Pious, Minerva, 187
Pittman, Frank, 66, 68, 118
Pitts, Zasu, 118-21
"Plot to Overthrow Christmas, The", 265
Popeye the Sailor, 205-6
Preminger, Otto, 207
Prentiss, Ed, 58, 77
Price, Vincent, 54, 55, 266
Promise & the Performance, The, 304
Provine, Dorothy, 253

Q
Quinn, Don, 105, 118

R
Radio Communications Company, 6
Radio Days, 99
Radio Hilversum, 10
Radio Luxembourg, 37
Radulovich, Lieutenant Milo, 293-4
Raggedy Ann, 206
Randolph, Isabel, 114

Randolph, Lillian, 199
Rayburn, Gene, 215
Red Channels, 296
Real Life Stories, 198
Red Ryder, 229
Red Skelton Show, The, 83
Reinhardt, Alice, 82, 89
Reinhardt, Django, 11
Reluctant Dragon, The, 233
Remarkable Miss Tuttle, The, 199
Rifleman, The, 83
Roaring Twenties, The, 253, 254
Robb, Mary Lee, 69
Robinson, Edward G., 33
Robson, William N. (Bill), 307
Rodman, Victor, 270
Rogers, Roy, 229
Rogers, Will, 305, 308
Romance, 233, 234, 238, 240, 242
Romance of Helen Trent, The, 75, 76
Romero, Cesar, 45
Roosevelt, Franklin D., 305, 313
Ross, Earle, 69
Roundtree, Martha, 182
Russell, Andy, 79
Ryan, Quinn, 74
Rye, Michael, 78, 268

S
Saint George and the Dragon, 134
Sarnoff, David, 303, 308, 309, 310, 317
Say One for Me, 85
Scaramouche, 250
Schorr, Daniel, 301
Schwartz, Dave, 34
Schwarzenegger, Arnold, 209
Science in the News, 97, 98
Scooby Doo Movies, The New, 99

Screen Guild Theatre, 99
Sears Radio Theatre, 266
Secombe, Harry, 9, 14, 16, 20
Secret Agent X-9, 74
See it Now, 291, 293, 320, 321
Sellers, Peter, 9, 14, 16, 18, 19, 20, 36
Sentimental Banker, The (Bob and Ray), 216
Sesame Street, 99
Sevareid, Eric, 283, 301
Seymour, Jane, 254
Shadow, The, 49, 58, 79, 200
Shane, 229
Shaw, George Bernard, 313
Shazzan, 82
Sherman, Ransom, 114, 128, 269
Shirer, William L., 282, 283, 284, 307, 312
Sidney, Sylvia, 182
Simon & Simon, 99
Simon, Al, 41, 47
Sinatra, Frank, 207-8
Six Shooter, The, 229
Skelton, Red, 196, 257
Skinner, Edna, 42
Skippy, 76
Slater, Ruth, 59
Smackout, 105, 106
Small World, 297
Smile Parade, 129
Smith Family, The, 105, 118
Smith, Howard K., 301
Smurfs, The, 47
Solomon, Leo, 34
Sommers, Jay, 35, 269
Soulé, Olan, 55, 57, 77, 87-99, 101, 268, 270

Sperber, Ann, 277-302
Stag Party, 30
Stang, Arnold, 31, 32, 183, 190-1, 197-209, 221
Stanton, Frank, 314, 315
Stapleton, Maureen, 207
Stewart, James 'Jimmy', 229
Strindberg, August, 232
Studebaker, Hugh, 93
Sugar Babies, 208
Sunday Dinner at Aunt Fanny's, 129
Sunday Times, The, 13
Support Your Local Gunfighter, 255
Suspense, 233, 240, 244

T

Tales from the Darkside, 20
Temperature's Rising, 251-2
Tenney Building, 52
Tetley, Walter, 31, 69, 71, 252
That Brewster Boy, 199
That Was the Week That Was, 135, 193, 194
Thin Man, The, 80
This Gun for Hire, 233
This is Your FBI, 259
Thompson, Bill, 107, 111, 112, 114, 125
Those Websters, 60, 61-3, 263, 268
Thurber, James, 192
Tillstrom, Burr, 130, 131, 133-5, 136, 194
Time Machine, 48
Tisch, Laurence A. 'Larry', 317, 318
Tobacco Road, 207
Today's Children, 53, 54
Todd, John, 65, 92
Tom Mix, 58, 59, 229
Tom Thumb, 36

Top Cat, 205-6, 209
Toscanini, Arturo, 198
Tracy, Spencer, 229
Tremayne, Les, 29, 57, 73-85, 94, 101, 268
Tremayne's, The, 82
Trendle, George W., 65
Tucker, Richard, 59
Turner III, Robert Edward 'Ted', 317
Tuttle, Lurene, 58, 69
Twilight Zone, 99

U

Uncle Quinn's Scallywags, 74, 89
United Independent Broadcasters, 305
Untouchables, The, 274

V

Ventura, Ray, 11, 12
Vic and Sade, 60
Video Theatre, 83
Virginian, The, 83, 251

W

W9XYZ, 82
Wait Until Your Father Comes Home, 206
Waldo, Janet, 265
Walliser, Blair, 74
War and Remembrance, 234
War of the Worlds, The, 84, 306
Warner, Gertrude, 79
Warner, Jack, 253
Waterman, Willard, 51-72, 77, 101, 262, 263
Webb, Jane, 60
Webb, Richard 'Dick', 93
Weber, Henry, 95
Weber, Marian, 59, 80

Webster, Carl, 53
Weinrott, Les, 130
Welk, Lawrence, 126
Welles, Orson, 89, 200, 275, 306
WENR, 117
West, Mae, 39
West, Paul, 66
Western Electric Company, 6
WGN, 75, 83, 304
WHA, 52, 105
What's My Line, 202
WHDH, 211
Whistler, The, 263
White, Andy, 66
Whiteman, Paul, 311
WHN, 217
WIBA, 51
WIBO, 104
Wilcox, Harlow, 120
Wild, Wild West, 255
William Morris Agency, 66
Windmill Theatre, 14
Windom, William, 192
Winds of War, 254
WLS, 117-8
WLW, 304
WMAQ, 98
WMCA, 181
WMT, 123
Woman in My House, The, 73
Wood, Natalie, 2275
Wood, Robert, 316
Woodson, William, 270
WOR, 304
Wouk, Herman, 254
Wright, Ben, 44, 235, 238, 245
Wyman, Thomas H. 'Tom', 317, 318

Wynn, Ed, 34

Y

Young Lions, The, 272
Young, Alan, 29-48, 184, 187, 201-2
Young, Carleton, 240, 270
Young, Rush, 91

Your Hit Parade, 70
Yours Truly, Johnny Dollar, 238, 240, 260-2

Z

Zenkl, Mayor Petr (Prague), 288
Zero Hour, 244
Zukor, Adolph, 307-8

www.ingramcontent.com/pod-product-compliance
Lightning Source LLC
Chambersburg PA
CBHW060552230426
43670CB00011B/1786